INSIGHT  GUIDES

D0982208

ST LUCIA
POCKET GUIDE

www.insightguides.com/StLucia

◉ Walking Eye App

Your Insight Pocket Guide purchase includes a free download of the destination's corresponding eBook. It is available now from the free Walking Eye container app in the App Store and Google Play. Simply download the Walking Eye container app to access the eBook dedicated to your purchased book. The app also features free information on local events taking place and activities you can enjoy during your stay, with the option to book them. In addition, premium content for a wide range of other destinations is available to purchase in-app.

HOW TO DOWNLOAD THE WALKING EYE APP

Available on purchase of this guide only.

1. Visit our website: www.insightguides.com/walkingeye
2. Download the Walking Eye container app to your smartphone (this will give you access to your free eBook and the ability to purchase other products)
3. Select the scanning module in the Walking Eye container app
4. Scan the QR Code on this page – you will be asked to enter a verification word from the book as proof of purchase
5. Download your free eBook* for travel information on the go

* Other destination apps and eBooks are available for purchase separately or are free with the purchase of the Insight Guide book

TOP 10 ATTRACTIONS

GRAND ANSE
This huge expanse of sand on the northeast coast is one of the best places for turtle watching. See page 49.

ST LUCIA DISTILLERS
The rum distillery showcases traditional and modern methods of producing this iconic Caribbean spirit. See page 53.

EDMUND FOREST RESERVE
Hike and birdwatch with a forest ranger. See page 91.

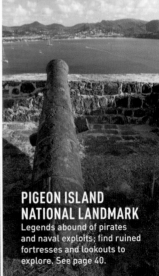

PIGEON ISLAND NATIONAL LANDMARK
Legends abound of pirates and naval exploits; find ruined fortresses and lookouts to explore. See page 40.

ANSE CHASTENET
Snorkel or dive to see the colourful reef in the marine reserve. See page 61.

THE PITONS
These iconic twin peaks feature on every postcard. See page 69.

CASTRIES CENTRAL MARKET
Vendors sell a huge variety of island produce – including fruit, vegetables, spices and flowers – in and around the old iron building. See page 31.

CAP MOULE À CHIQUE
Climb to the lighthouse for a panoramic view of the island. See page 75.

MARIA ISLANDS NATURE RESERVE
Tiny islands offshore are home to rare reptiles and nesting seabirds. See page 76.

MAMIKU GARDENS
A delightful botanical garden for lovers of flowers and herbs. See page 79.

A PERFECT DAY

7.30am

Breakfast
Start the day with a good breakfast, including a selection of seasonal tropical fruits, including mango, papaya and pineapple, and juices such as fresh passion-fruit, guava or soursop, followed by banana bread and cocoa tea.

Noon

Plas Kassav
This is a great place to stop for a snack of the local cassava bread when driving down the west coast, before continuing on this scenic route which boasts photo opportunities around every curve.

8.30am

Castries
Start an island tour with a stop in the capital, visiting the market to pick up edible souvenirs such as cocoa, spices or hot sauces. Wander around the harbour to see the variety of boats and ships and stroll across Derek Walcott Square to the Cathedral.

10.00am

Distillers
With prior reservation you can tour the rum distillery and learn how rum has been made for centuries. Finish with a tasting of some 20 different rums, which are also available to buy.

1.00pm

Soufrière
There is a range of rest-aurants here where you can sample fresh, locally-sourced ingredients at all budgets. A delicious creole lunch can be taken in town at Orlando's if you've made a reser-vation, or choose a more scenic option such as Boucan, overlooking the Pitons, where every dish has cacao in it.

4.00pm

Anse de Sables

Stretch your legs with a walk along the sand – or maybe even a dip in the sea – before stopping for a drink at the beach café, where you can admire the view over to the Maria Islands. Then head up the east coast back to Castries.

10.00pm

On the town

You can bar crawl through Rodney Bay, where there is usually some live music or other entertainment on. Or, if it is Friday, move on to the Gros Islet Jump-up for a lively street party that goes on until the small hours to the beat of reggae, soca and calypso.

2.00pm

Volcano

Pay a short visit to see the bubbling mud and steaming vents of Soufrière's 'drive-in' volcano before continuing down to the south coast, stopping at La Fargue Craft Centre near Choiseul, taking a peek at the fishing village of Laborie and skirting the airport at Vieux Fort.

6.00pm

Cocktails

Brown Sugar at Vigie Cove is a good place for a sundowner after the long drive, as well as an enjoyable dinner, if you can't stir yourself.

8.00pm

Dinner

Rodney Bay is the place for dinner. Wander along the strip until you find whatever takes your fancy – from curry to flame-grilled lobster, the choice is wide.

CONTENTS

INTRODUCTION

Every year, several hundred thousand people visit the tiny island of St Lucia (pronounced *Loo-sha*) for the archetypal Caribbean holiday of sun, sea and sand, but soon discover a wealth of other attractions to enjoy. The Caribbean coast has long stretches of fine sand and healthy coral reefs, while the Atlantic-buffeted side provides good windsurfing and has nature reserves populated by rare wildlife as well as extensive stretches of sand, remote from mass tourism and popular with nesting turtles. At the island's heart the land is lush with trees, and there are forest reserves in the mountains and on the Pitons, the landmark twin, cone-shaped peaks. St Lucia is stunningly beautiful.

LANDSCAPE

Lying at the southern end of the Lesser Antilles chain, St Lucia is part of the Windward Islands group, with Martinique 34km (21 miles) to the north, St Vincent 34km (21 miles) to the south and Barbados 160km (100 miles) to the southeast. The island comprises 617 sq km (238 sq miles) of undulating hills and mountains covered with native trees, coconut palms, banana plantations and several types of forest. The second-largest of the Windward Islands group – only Dominica is bigger – volcanic St Lucia is 43km (27 miles) long and 22km (14 miles) wide, with beaches of black or golden sand, hot sulphur springs, a scenic mountain range and rich, fertile soil. St Lucia has a tropical, humid climate that provides warm sunshine most of the year, cooled by northeastern trade winds. Showers at any time of year keep the land lush and green.

Foreign flowers

Flowering trees such as the immortelle or African tulip tree provide bursts of colour but are not native to St Lucia.

Castries locals

PEOPLE AND HERITAGE

The island population of about 174,000, is a pot pourri of people of African, Amerindian, European and East Indian descent. European settlement, indentured labour and slavery helped to determine the ethnic mix of the country. Disease, war and colonisation contributed to the disappearance of the island's Amerindian population, which was virtually wiped out by the time enslaved Africans were introduced in the late 17th-century. Few people can trace their ancestry directly to the Kalinago, who inhabited the island at the time of colonisation. However, there are St Lucians who are of mixed African and Amerindian blood.

People with an African heritage are likely to be descendants of the slaves brought as forced labour to work the land, while St Lucians of European heritage are probably the descendants of settlers, plantation owners and poor white labourers. There are also descendants of East Indian indentured labourers who arrived after the abolition of slavery. Today, around 80 percent of the population is of African origin, under 3 percent of East Indian extraction, with 12 percent of mixed heritage, and people of European origin making up the remainder. This is a Creole society in its broadest sense: a rich and rare combination of races, cultures, languages and cuisine.

LANGUAGE AND CULTURE

Although St Lucia has been a British territory since 1814 and the official language is English, French culture pervades. A melodic French Creole (Kwéyòl) is spoken by more than 90 percent of people in informal arenas and, due to a drive to preserve and promote Creole traditions, is increasingly used in official circles as well. It has been suggested that a large percentage of children do not speak English until they go to school. Efforts are being made to hold on to the rich Creole folklore, music and language. There are annual festivals, which include traditional

THE KWÉYÒL TONGUE

Kwéyòl began as an oral language that initially helped the French and groups from different parts of the African continent communicate effectively. It was derived from elements of French, a variety of African vocabulary and grammar, English and a little Spanish. St Lucian Kwéyòl did not have an official written form until the 20th century and today many people who are fluent Kwéyòl speakers are not literate in the language. Kwéyòl continues to gain legitimacy through the work of community groups and increasingly published literature. In 1998 Kwéyòl was officially recognised in the St Lucia House of Assembly and in 1999 the New Testament was published in Kwéyòl, a project that took 15 years to complete, followed in 2001 by a Kwéyòl dictionary.

storytellers, folk singers and carnival masqueraders.

The French influence can be seen in place and family names and also in the island's closeness to the neighbouring French *département* of Martinique. There are common linguistic elements in St Lucian and Martinican Creole. However, St Lucian Kwéyòl isn't as close to the French language as one might imagine.

A cocoa pod at Fondoux

The French influence can also be seen in religion. Over two thirds of islanders are Roman Catholic and the church plays an important part in the lives of ordinary people. However, living by traditional Christian values hasn't prevented St Lucians from retaining elements of the old West African belief system and folklore – *obeah*. An *obeah* man or woman works spells and creates potions from roots and other forest plants that can heal or harm. However, they are better known for creating mischief.

Before the advent of modern medicine the healing practitioner was sought out to cure illnesses, using ancient herbal remedies. Today, people are turning back to nature in an attempt to recoup knowledge about the medicinal properties of native plants, which flourish in the wild and in domestic gardens.

ENVIRONMENT AND WILDLIFE

St Lucia has a thriving forest covering 77 sq km (30 sq miles), although a large proportion of was cut down for plantation crops in colonial times. Much of the remaining rainforest is protected now to safeguard the island's water supply and

St Lucia is home to lush landscapes

wildlife. Fresh water cascades through the mountains, the rivers and streams feeding the land below.

Rare birds and wildlife include the national bird, the St Lucian parrot, the St Lucia oriole, the red-billed tropic bird and the St Lucia black finch. Nature trails through the forest may also reveal the agouti, a guinea pig-like creature, an iguana or a mongoose. Native to the island are the boa constrictor and the poisonous fer-de-lance snake, rarely seen because the creatures populate the dry scrub areas on the east coast not usually explored by walkers.

On the west coast are the fertile valleys of Roseau and Cul de Sac where many of the banana plantations are located. In contrast, the north side is drier, with cacti proliferating.

St Lucia has been mindful to preserve the natural environment that attracts many visitors and provides a livelihood for local fishermen. Divers and snorkellers flock to the diverse sea life of the coral reefs that border the western and southern areas of the island.

A BRIEF HISTORY

St Lucia's ancient history is shrouded in mystery and our knowledge of the peoples who lived there before the arrival of Europeans at the beginning of the 16th century, is based on recent archaeological and anthropological investigations. What is certain, however, is that this lush and fertile island attracted waves of immigrants from South America, heading up the arc of islands from what is now Trinidad to the Greater Antilles, and some of them put down roots and stayed.

ST LUCIA'S FIRST INHABITANTS

The first settlers on St Lucia were Amerindians travelling up the island chain by canoe from the Orinoco region of South America around AD 200. Settlements have been discovered on neighbouring islands which pre-date this arrival, so it is possible that people lived on the island before then, but no evidence has yet been found. The earliest archaeological remains have been found at Grand Anse on the east coast, as well as at Anse Noir in the south near Vieux Fort.

These migrants are referred to as Island Arawaks because they came from an area on the continent where the language, Arawak, was spoken. They would have had another name for themselves but that has got lost over time. Some time

BRITISH MODEL OF GOVERNMENT

St Lucia is governed by a multi-party parliamentary democracy based on the British model and led by an elected prime minister. A House of Assembly made up of 17 members is elected for a five-year term and the island's Governor General appoints the 11-member Senate.

around 1450, a further flow of migration brought the Caribs, who called themselves Kalinago, and the Island Arawaks disappeared. It is not known whether they left, were killed or absorbed into the invading culture, but they ceased making their pottery after that date.

When the Spanish arrived at the beginning of the 16th century, the Kalinago were the sole occupants of the island they called Iouanalao, meaning 'where the iguana is found'. The name later morphed into Hiwanarau and then Hewanorra, a title now given to the international airport in the south.

EUROPEAN COLONISATION

Further mystery surrounds the arrival of the Spanish. Although legend had it that Christopher Columbus discovered

An example of Bellin's rare 1758 map of Saint Lucia

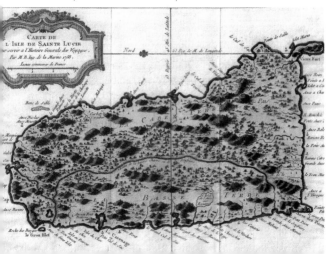

the island on St Lucy's Day (13 December) in 1502, his ship's log showed he wasn't even in the area on that day. Despite not knowing who discovered the island, nor when, St Lucy's Day has been adopted as the national holiday. Someone must have spotted it, though, as in 1520, a Vatican globe marked it as Santa Lucía, implying that it was claimed by Spain. It is believed that in the 1550s, the pirate François Le Clerc, or Jambe de Bois, tried to settle on the island and

Arawak woman by John Gabriel Stedman

there may later have been an attempt by a Dutch expedition. In 1605, an English ship, *Olive Branch*, landed at Vieux Fort after being blown off course en route to Guiana (Guyana). Of the 67 survivors only 19 were left a month later, when they escaped in a dugout canoe. The Kalinago did not take kindly to unwelcome visitors.

In 1627, St Lucia appeared in a document as one of the territories granted to the Earl of Carlisle. There were no immediate attempts to settle the land and in 1635, the French made a counter-claim that the land had been granted to M. d'Esnambuc by Cardinal Richelieu in 1626. This was the beginning of a territorial dispute between England and France which was to last until 1814, during which time the island changed hands 14 times.

In 1638 the English made a serious attempt to settle St Lucia, with an expedition comprising 300 men from Bermuda

A Carib, or Kalinago family

and St Kitts. They managed to live alongside the Kalinago for 18 months until a dispute in 1640 lead to many deaths on both sides and the English survivors fled. Three years later, the French appointed a governor who was married to an Amerindian, allowing him to make peace and establish the first permanent settlement. Around this time, the King of France ceded the island to the French West India Company, who in 1650 sold it to MM Houel and Du Parquet. The English continued to state their claim and the two nations began to fight over the island, all the while being harassed by the Kalinago, who tried to get rid of the settlers and killed several governors. Gradually, however, the settlers, who were mostly French, introduced a plantation economy using slave labour, growing first cocoa and coffee and then sugar.

EUROPEAN WARFARE

St Lucia was one of many islands that were fought over by European powers in the 17th and 18th centuries, being caught up in strategic manoeuvres of governments from far away. While the Spanish were interested in the Greater Antilles, particularly Cuba, for its position on the shipping route between Spain, South and Central America, the English, French and Dutch battled mostly over the Lesser Antilles.

One of the most famous battles was in 1782, when Admiral George Rodney led the English fleet from Pigeon Island to attack the French navy off the islands of Les Saintes, intercepting it on its way to attack Jamaica.

The French Revolution, which began in 1789, also had implications for the French colonies, particularly when the new French Republic granted freedom to enslaved Africans in its overseas territories in 1794. Victor Hugues supported insurrections in neighbouring islands from his base in St Lucia. The guillotine was erected in Castries and the island became known as St Lucie La Fidèle by the French. In 1796, General Sir Ralph Abercrombie led English troops in another invasion, fighting a long campaign against a joint force of white and black Republicans. The newly emancipated islanders, fearing they would be returned to bondage, banded together, joined by a number of French army deserters, to create l'Armée Française dans les Bois. The

Rodney attacking the French fleet in 1782

rebels – called Brigands by their enemies – led a campaign of resistance across the island. In 1795 they took control of the fortifications on Pigeon Island, but victory was short-lived. In 1796 British forces defeated and captured them at Morne Fortuné.

The Treaty of Amiens in 1802, which ended the Seven Years' War, returned St Lucia to the French, before it was finally ceded to the British in the Treaty of Paris in 1814. Despite the ideals of the French Revolution, slavery remained in force on St Lucia until the British passed the Emancipation Act in 1834, which came into force in 1838.

BRITISH RULE

From 1838, St Lucia came under the jurisdiction of the Windward Islands Government, with a Governor based first in

Locals carrying coal onboard a U.S. warship at Castries, 1903

Barbados and then in Grenada. While important as a plantation economy, from 1885, St Lucia experienced a period of prosperity when it became an important coaling station. Welsh coal was sold to passing steam ships and by the end of the century, Castries was the 14th most important port in the world when rated by tonnage handled. The rise

Workers' champion

George Frederick Lawrence Charles came to prominence in 1945 when he championed the cause of striking construction workers who were employed to build an extension to the airport. Knighted in 1998, the airport in Castries was renamed in his honour and a sculpture of the trade unionist was erected there in 2002.

of oil, however, saw the decline of steam ships and a fall in demand for coal, with a resulting adverse impact on the colony's economy.

The 1930s were a period of poverty and labour unrest. In 1935 coal workers went on strike and there was violence which had to be put down by the navy. Two years later sugar workers also came out on strike demanding higher wages. This was the beginning of an organised labour movement, culminating in the formation of the first trade union in 1939: the St Lucia Workers Co-Operative Union. This later grew into the St Lucia Labour Party (SLP), led by George FL Charles (1916–2004), who had championed striking workers and became the secretary of the Union, a reformer and one of the most important politicians of the 20th century.

In 1951, universal adult suffrage was introduced for the first time and elections that year were won by the SLP. Charles became the first Chief Minister and retained power until 1964. He introduced legislation improving workers' rights and oversaw the shift from sugar production, which had been hit by falling prices, to bananas, which could be

Banana farmer

produced on smallholdings, benefiting large numbers of small scale farmers. In 1958, St Lucia joined the short-lived West Indies Federation, until it collapsed in 1961, when Jamaica pulled out.

The 1964 elections were won by the United Workers Party (UWP), led by John Compton (1925–2007), another prominent politician of the late 20th century. He held power from 1964 to 1979, and won subsequent elections in 1982, 1987 and 1992, before retiring in 1996. However, Compton came out of retirement to lead the UWP to victory in the 2006 elections, beating the SLP which had lost popularity during difficult economic times and becoming Prime Minister aged 82, a position he held until his death a year later.

During his first period of office, St Lucia gained full internal self-government, becoming a State in voluntary association with Britain. Full independence was gained in 1979. St Lucia remains a member of the Commonwealth with Queen Elizabeth II as head of state, represented by the Governor General.

CHALLENGES IN THE 21ST CENTURY

Although St Lucia has the largest banana crop in the Windward Islands and has diversified into other agricultural products, such as renovating historic cacao plantations, planting coconuts, growing flowers and promoting fisheries, farming alone is insufficient to sustain the island's economy. Entrepreneurs have gradually turned to tourism, which has been promoted by the government to provide jobs as well as bring in foreign exchange. The spectacular landscape of the Pitons, declared a UNESCO World Heritage Site in 2005, marinas, plenty of sandy beaches and other natural features attract some 320,000 stayover tourists and 600,000 cruise ship passengers a year. Investment in hotels has been

FAIRTRADE BANANAS

Banana growers in the Windward Islands benefit from the Fairtrade scheme. It enables small farm owners to pay decent wages to their workers and protect their environment without resorting to heavy use of agrochemicals. They produce less than half the quantity of bananas per hectare produced in the intensive, corporate-owned plantations of Latin America, but in the fragile island ecosystems such levels of output would be unsustainable. At a time when international competition is fierce, with the end of EU quotas because of WTO rulings, the Fairtrade scheme is vital to the survival of St Lucian banana farmers. In 2007, Sainsbury's supermarket in the UK announced that all the bananas it sells would be fairly traded and that 100 million, or 75 percent of the total crop, would come from St Lucia.

significant, from low budget guest houses to the height of luxury at sky-high prices.

Nevertheless, the industry remains at the mercy of the world economy and suffered from the international financial crisis of 2008 and thereafter, when the slowdown and high oil prices affected travel. With the fiscal deficit running at nearly 10 per cent of gross domestic product, there is little leeway for the government to soften the impact of external factors with greater spending at home.

In a bid to secure sustainable sources of energy, in 2014 the government began negotiations with the World Bank and the government of New Zealand to develop a geothermal project at Soufrière. If successful, this project has the potential to provide investment and jobs as well as generate electricity and stabilise energy prices on the island for years to come.

Cruise ships docked in Castries

HISTORICAL LANDMARKS

AD 200 Amerindians arrive in canoes from the north of South America.

1450 The Kalinago (Caribs) migrate from South America and take over the island.

1502 Columbus may have sighted St Lucia.

1550s The pirate, François Le Clerc, tried to settle St Lucia.

1605 The English land in the south after a ship is blown off course.

1627 Land granted to the Earl of Carlisle includes St Lucia.

1635 The French establish a colony, claiming the island was granted to M. d'Esnambuc in 1626.

1638 300 Englishmen from Bermuda and St Kitts settle on St Lucia but flee after 18 months because of battles with the Kalinago.

1659 The English and French commence hostilities. The island changes hands 14 times in 150 years.

1782 Admiral Rodney destroys the French fleet at the Battle of Les Saintes.

1814 St Lucia is ceded to Britain in the Treaty of Paris.

1838 Following the Act of Emancipation in 1834, slavery is abolished in British territories.

1885 Castries becomes a major coaling station selling coal to passing steam ships.

1920s The rise of oil and decline of coal lead to economic problems for St Lucia.

1930s Poor working conditions and strikes for higher wages lead to the formation of the first trade union.

1951 Universal adult suffrage is established in the British colonies.

1967 St Lucia gains internal self-government as a State in voluntary association with Great Britain.

1979 St Lucia gains full independence.

2005 The Pitons are declared a UNESCO World Heritage site.

2014 Negotiations begin with the World Bank and New Zealand to develop geothermal energy at Soufrière.

WHERE TO GO

The majority of places to stay in St Lucia are concentrated in two areas: in the northwest at Rodney Bay and in the south-west around Soufrière. The former is the place to go for beach activities, marina and nightlife. The latter has spectacular views of the Pitons, surrounded by rainforest, with equally beautiful underwater life. There are lots of excursions on offer from the north to visit attractions in the south overland or by sea, but fewer going the other way. It is feasible to drive around most of the island in a day, stopping along the way to visit a few attractions, take photos and find somewhere pleasant for lunch. Hiring a driver is more relaxing than driving yourself on mountain roads, with the benefit of learning more about the island from a knowledgeable guide.

CASTRIES AND ENVIRONS

St Lucia's capital, **Castries ❶**, which lies on the western side of the island, has a population of 67,000. It has been razed by fire and rebuilt four times over the years, leaving few old buildings with historic or architectural value. Much of the town is made up of nondescript modern buildings, but Castries still has character and vibrancy, especially on Saturday when the market is awash with local people doing their weekly shopping and curious tourists enjoying the atmosphere and searching for souvenirs. If there are cruise ships in port, then Castries bulges at the seams.

A local staple

Cassava is a root vegetable grown throughout St Lucia. The plant is peeled and grated and the juice extracted, before it is dried to produce farine (a fine flour), which is used to make bread or porridge.

St Lucia is home to many luxury resorts, as here at Piton Bay

The Port of Castries is a busy working harbour where container ships can be seen unloading their contents on to the dock at the North Wharf, adjacent to the Place Carenage duty-free shopping mall. When cruise ships are in the harbour they dominate all other vessels and even the surrounding buildings. Fishing boats painted the colours of the rainbow can be seen dodging the big ships to get in and out of their harbour in Trou Garnier, while yachts sail in and out of Petit Carenage.

A tour of Castries is best negotiated on foot, as the central area is compact, but a taxi is recommended when you explore the sights such as Morne Fortune on the southern outskirts. Buses are also readily available.

THE TOWN CENTRE

Derek Walcott Square  sits at the heart of the capital bordered by Brazil, Laborie, Micoud and Bourbon streets. This well-kept, small green space scattered with a few mature trees, was called Place d'Armes in the 18th century, when it was the site of public executions around the time of the French Revolution. By the late 20th century, the square had undergone two name changes: it was called Columbus Square until 1993, when it was renamed in honour of

Castries' waterfront

Castries-born poet and playwright Derek Walcott, who won the Nobel Prize for Literature in 1992.

A tall samaan tree with branches laden with epiphytes is believed to be more than 400 years old and offers some shady relief from the tropical sun. A paved pathway runs through the middle linking a memorial obelisk and plaque to the bandstand at the opposite end. The memorial at the west side of the square honours the memory of St Lucians who fought and died in both World Wars. 'Jazz on the Square' is a popular event that attracts visitors and locals who gather here for a

daily dose of free music during the St Lucia Jazz Festival, held in May. Office workers often use the bandstand and benches here during their lunch hour. At the centre of the square is a fountain and a little way back towards the bandstand are busts of the island's two Nobel Prize winners: Derek Walcott and economist Sir Arthur Lewis.

On the corner of Laborie and Micoud streets is the Roman Catholic cathedral **The Minor Basilica of the Immaculate Conception** ❸ (open daily unless Mass is in progress). This has been the site of several churches dating back to the 18th century, but the current building was not completed until 1931. The cathedral's exterior is shabby, but inside there are enough beautiful dark wood pews to seat around 2,000, intricately carved columns and arches, and a stone altar flanked by displays of votive candles, which can also be found near

HONOURABLE ST LUCIAN

Born in Castries in 1930, Derek Walcott OBE OCC trained as a painter and writer and studied at the University of the West Indies in Jamaica. In 1953 he moved to Trinidad where, in 1959, he founded the Trinidad Theatre Workshop. In 1981 he set up the Boston Playwrights Theatre at Boston University, where he worked as Professor of Literature. Since 2010 he has been Professor of Poetry at the University of Essex in the UK, although he spends much of his time in St Lucia. He has published many collections of poems, an autobiography in verse, *Another Life*, critical works and over 20 plays. His works include the epic narrative poem, *Omeros* (1990), which contributed to him winning the Nobel Prize for Literature in 1992. In 2011 he won the TS Eliot Prize for his book of poetry, *White Egrets* (2010). His twin, Roderick, was also a playwright, poet and artist, and their childhood home on Grass Street has been declared a heritage site.

the cathedral's side altars. Yellow light floods the building via decorative windows in the ceiling, which is adorned with a depiction of Catholic saints. Renowned St Lucian artist, Dunstan St Omer, painted the murals on the cathedral walls in 1985 in preparation for a visit by Pope John Paul II the following year. The beautiful paintings reveal the Stations of the Cross with charac-

Castries Central Market is the best place to find crafts and food

ters inspired by local people. In 2005, St Omer and his son, Giovanni, created 12 magnificent stained glass windows that were installed on either side of the cathedral.

As you leave the cathedral on Laborie Street, to your left is Brazil Street, which has several buildings dating back to the late 19th century. Though fading, the wooden structures retain some lovely gingerbread fretwork detail on their balconies. These and the buildings behind were the only ones of their kind to survive Castries' last great fire in 1948.

One of the only other places to escape the flames in 1948 was the old **Central Market** **C** situated north of Jeremie Street towards John Compton Highway. Built of iron in 1894, the original market shelter is where you will find the town clock and a modern annexe. Vendors from rural areas sell local produce, such as fruit, vegetables, cassava, cocoa sticks, pepper sauces, spices and basketwork.

Across the road on Peynier Street is the **Vendors' Arcade** **D**, which backs on to the waterfront; you can find an array of souvenirs and gifts including inexpensive, colourful T-shirts, beach wraps and some very good basketwork, in both traditional and modern styles.

Head west from the Arcade along Jeremie Street to **La Place Carenage** **E** (Mon–Fri 9am–5pm, Sat 9am–2pm, also Sun if a cruise ship is in town), the duty-free shopping mall, with a selection of shops selling crafts and souvenirs, boutiques and art galleries. The mall also has a small interpretative facility, the **Desmond Skeete Animation Centre**, which has displays of ancient Amerindian artefacts and an audio tour. Heading west along La Toc Road you come to the ferry terminal, from where the L'Express des Iles ferry operates a regular and fast service to Martinique, Dominica, Guadeloupe and the outer French islands.

VIGIE PENINSULA **2**

Across the harbour and reached by a regular water taxi service is the large, upscale **Pointe Seraphine** **F** duty-free shopping mall (Mon–Sat 9am–5pm, also Sun if a cruise ship is in town), busy at the weekend and even more so when a cruise ship is anchored at the dock next door. Take the inexpensive ferry to cross the water or jump in a taxi for the short drive around the harbour. The walk from here to Castries centre isn't that long, but it can seem so, especially in the heat. On the Vigie peninsula is the **George F.L. Charles Airport** (formerly known as Vigie Airport), a small landing

19th-century, colonial style, wooden buildings overlooking Derek Walcott Square

Vigie Lighthouse offers a fantastic position from which to see much of the island, as well as Martinique

strip for Caribbean inter-island and domestic flights. As you round the corner to join Peninsular Road, with the airport runway on your left, you will see the raised white tombstones and monuments in the small military cemetery created for the men of the West India Regiment. Vigie Beach runs alongside the road on the right. The entire peninsula was once a military stronghold and the barracks and other 19th century military buildings have been restored.

Vigie Lighthouse G stands at the end of Beacon Road on the peninsula, on the northern side of the city harbour. The light from the red lantern at the top of the 11m (36ft) white tower, built in 1914, can be seen about 50km (30 miles) out to sea. The lighthouse overlooks military barracks, 18th-century ruins and other historic buildings managed by the National Trust. From here on a clear day there are spectacular views of the southern and northern coasts, and Martinique.

THE MORNE ❸

The historic Morne area is accessible from the southern end of the centre of Castries. On the way up is the studio and shop of **Bagshaws of St Lucia** (Mon–Fri 8.30am–4pm; tours Sat–Sun by appointment; tel: 758-452 6039). The factory uses traditional silk-screen methods to produce colourful prints on fabric, with motifs inspired by island flora and fauna. Tours provide a lively explanation of the printing process and details about Bagshaws. The company also has shopping outlets at La Carenage and Pointe Seraphine in Castries, and another at Hewanorra Airport.

Next door, Bagshaws have restored **La Toc Battery** (tours by appointment; tel: 758-452 6039), a fine example of a 19th-century battlement with wonderful views and a pretty garden. Built by the British, La Toc has cannons, underground tunnels and munitions storage rooms where valuable artefacts can be seen. There is also a display of some 900 old bottles and other artefacts, found by scuba divers in Castries' harbour.

On top of the hill is the 29-hectare (72-acre) **Morne Fortune Historic Area ⓗ**, where you will find the old military buildings of **Fort Charlotte**. The French began building the original fortress in 1768, choosing 260m (850ft) high Morne Fortune because of its unmatched vantage point of the harbour. When they took control of St Lucia in 1814, the British continued the work and strengthened the fortifications. It was they who named it Fort Charlotte. The fort remained an important defensive base until early in the 20th century. The military barracks and

Sir Arthur Lewis

St Lucia is proud to have produced two Nobel Laureates, the first of whom, Sir Arthur Lewis (1915–1991), was awarded his prize for Economics in 1979 for his theories on development economics.

The Powder Magazine and Guard Cells are the oldest existing buildings on Morne Fortune

other buildings have been restored and converted. Some now house the Sir Arthur Lewis Community College, named after the island's first Nobel Prize winner, who is buried here. Nearby are the ruins of Apostle's Battery, with a large mounted cannon, built in 1890 to support the fortress, as well as the lookout point at Prevost's Redoubt, a French construction dating from 1782.

At the southern boundaries of the fort complex is the **Royal Inniskilling Fusiliers Memorial**, a monument to the soldiers who battled for this position against the Brigands and the French in 1796. The monument also marks one of the best viewpoints on the Morne, affording stunning coastal views to Pigeon Island in the north and as far as the Pitons on the west coast.

While in the area, it is worth visiting the Goodlands workshop of the St Lucian sculptor and woodcarver Vincent

Fisherman mending nets

Joseph Eudovic and his artistic family. At **Eudovic's Art Studio and Gallery** ❶ (Mon–Fri 7.30am–4.30pm, Sat–Sun until 3pm; tel: 758-452 2747; http://eudovicart. com) woodcarvers produce smooth abstract carvings. The works are made from the ancient roots and stumps of the laurier canelle, laurier mabouey, teak, mahogany and red and white cedar.

Howelton House, the home of **Caribelle Batik** ❶ (Mon–Fri 8am–4pm, Sat 8am–noon, Sun if a cruise ship is in port; tel: 758-452 3785; http://caribellebatikstlucia.com), is a fine example of Victorian architecture with a Caribbean twist. The pretty building on Old Victoria Road has been carefully restored and houses a batik studio and print shop, which uses Indonesian techniques to create vibrant designs on British and sea-island cotton. The fabric, printed with images of St Lucia's flora and fauna, such as colourful heliconia, is then made into clothing, wall hangings and souvenirs.

RODNEY BAY AND THE NORTH

The coastal region to the north of Castries is the island's foremost resort area with sheltered bays on the western, Caribbean side, a range of hotels, fishing communities, a marina, shopping malls, vibrant nightlife and historic land-marks. West of the highway, several hotels and restaurants nestle in the curve of **Choc Bay** and along Choc Beach, which is lapped by the calm waters of the Caribbean. Further north, in Bois d'Orange, residences and a hotel are scattered around the hill overlooking **Labrellotte Bay**.

RODNEY BAY ❹

Taking a left turn off the Castries-Gros Islet highway at the Bay Walk Mall on the left-hand side of the road will lead you to **Rodney Bay** ❻ village, where there is a bank with an ATM, lively bars, restaurants and small hotels. This is the hip strip for nightlife in St Lucia, being close to hotels, with food outlets serving simple sandwiches, pizza, steak, seafood and French, Indian, Italian and Caribbean cuisine. The hotels also organise entertainment such as crab racing, fire eaters, steel bands or jazz groups and several restaurants have live music on certain nights. The shopping in Rodney Bay is the best on the island. The Bay Walk Mall has a range of shops and a

Rodney Bay as seen from the hilltop of Pigeon Island National Park

Why Rodney Bay?

Rodney Bay is named after Admiral George Brydges Rodney, who claimed St Lucia for the British in 1762 and later established a naval base at nearby Pigeon Island, from where he set sail to intercept and defeat the French navy on its way to attack Jamaica in 1782.

casino. There is a supermarket there and in the older JQ Mall on the other side of the road and plenty of opportunities for sailors to provision their yachts.

At the end of the road is **Reduit Beach** ❶, one of the best stretches of sand on the island. The crescent-shaped beach extends as far as Pigeon Island (see page 40) further north, although it is not possible to walk the length of it because of shipping access to Rodney Bay marina and The Landings yacht harbour. There are lots of hotels here but there is public access to the beach, where visitors can rent watersports equipment, sun loungers and umbrellas. In high season, when the hotels are full, and at weekends, when local people visit the beach, it can become crowded, but there is usually enough space for everyone. If you are looking for tranquillity, come on a weekday in the off season. Licensed vendors work this beach, but if you are not interested in what they have to sell, a polite 'no thank you' is usually all it takes to discourage them.

Rodney Bay Marina ⓜ and its harbour were created by digging out a mangrove swamp. The popular marina is well equipped and is considered to be among the Caribbean's best. The **Atlantic Rally for Cruisers** (ARC) is a big winter event. Yachts from all over the world take part in this annual transatlantic rally, setting sail in November from Las Palmas in Gran Canaria to Rodney Bay in St Lucia. The 2,700-nautical mile journey takes anything from 12 to 24 days, and festivities around the marina continue as long as it takes for the vessels to reach their destination.

GROS ISLET ❺

Gros Islet  (pronounced *grows ee-lay*), just north of the marina, is a small fishing village that during the week is an antidote to the pace of the busy harbour. However, most visitors come to Gros Islet for the **Friday Night Jump-up**, a popular street party when tourists and locals converge on the area. Food and snack vendors line the usually quiet streets, bars and restaurants fling open their doors and sound systems flood the air with the beat of reggae, calypso and soca. This is a good place to enjoy tasty St Lucian dishes, such as locally caught fried fish, chicken or conch, then work off the calories by dancing the night away in the crowded street. Things don't hot up until after 10pm and festivities go on into the small hours. Generally it is pretty safe at the Jump-up, with police, uniformed and plain clothed, on duty, but keep your wits about you and always travel in a group.

Revellers at Gros Islet's Friday Night Jump-up

PIGEON ISLAND

Around the bay from Gros Islet is the **Pigeon Island National Landmark** ❻ (daily 9am–5pm; interpretative centre closed on Sun; entrance fee). This was once a separate island, accessible only by boat, but was joined to the mainland by a man-made causeway, completed in 1972, on which a few large resorts have been built. The resorts have claimed part of the sand for guests, but there is still a good stretch open to everyone. There is a small parking area and you can buy snacks from the vendors who trade close to the beach's public access point.

Cannon at Pigeon Island National Park

Operated by the St Lucia National Trust, Pigeon Island is of significant archaeological and historical importance. The hilly land that spans 18 hectares (45 acres) is thought to have been inhabited by Amerindians, who used the island's caves for shelter and grew staple crops such as sweet potatoes and cassava (manioc). In the 1550s, the pirate Jambe de Bois (Peg leg) also sheltered in the caves.

Later the site played its part during the 18th- and 19th-century squabbles between European imperialist powers over control of St Lucia. The island's strategic position and usefulness as a lookout made it a popular choice as a military base. Admiral Rodney established a naval outpost here in 1780. He sailed from this point to defeat the French forces two years later at the Battle of the Saints, which took place off the Iles des Saintes between Guadeloupe and Dominica. The Brigands (see page 19) captured the island and took control of the fortifications in 1795, forcing

Pigeon Island

the British to abandon St Lucia for a while, but it was retaken in 1798. From 1842 it was used as a quarantine centre, but abandoned by 1904.

By the early 20th century, Pigeon Island was leased to Napoleon Olivierre from St Vincent, who ran a whaling station. Later, in 1937, the island was leased to Josset Agnes Hutchinson, an actress with the D'Oyly Carte Opera company. There was a hiatus during World War II when the US established a communications station and a naval air station. In 1947 Hutchinson returned to her house in the south of the island (now a ruin), opening a beachfront restaurant, which attracted a colourful yachting crowd. She finally gave up the lease in 1970 and returned home to Britain in 1976.

Passing through the gates of the park you will be faced with a useful map of the area. The path to the right leads to the ruins of the **Officers' Kitchen** and a little further up the hill is the renovated **Officers' Mess**, which houses the small **Interpretative Centre**. Artefacts and historical displays explain the history and natural environment of Pigeon Island, but it is past its best.

The Ruins of Fort Rodney

The Officers' Mess is also home to the **St Lucia National Trust** (daily 8am–4pm; tel: 758-452 5005; www.slunatrust.org). The trust was established in 1975 as the result of a campaign to save the Pigeon Island Landmark from being used for a housing development. Its aim is to preserve the natural and cultural heritage of St Lucia, including areas of outstanding natural beauty, and bio-diverse and historic sites such as Pigeon Island, Fregate Island and Maria Islands. Contact the National Trust office for tours of their properties.

In late spring the park is a popular venue for the St Lucia Jazz Festival (see page 99). The stage is usually set up near the Officers' Mess, using the ocean as a beautiful backdrop; crowds arrive early to find a good spot on the grass from which to enjoy the show.

You can take a guided tour or simply wander along the paths and trails at leisure. There is a variety of flora, fauna and many old buildings, some no more than a collection of stones. On the waterfront, just before you reach the overgrown military cemetery, is the Jambe de Bois restaurant, a good choice for a drink, an ice cream or a snack. There is a jetty and ferry dock nearby and the lovely beach leads back almost level with the park border and entrance.

On a hill, at the southwestern tip of the park, are the ruins of **Fort Rodney**, which had an excellent vantage point. Today, the fort ruins still afford a good view south towards Castries, but the best lookout point is at 110m (361ft) **Signal Peak**.

It's a bit of a climb to reach the peak, especially in the hot sun, but it's worth it for the view over neighbouring Gros Islet and far north to the French island of Martinique. There is another lookout at the **Two-Gun Battery** close to the **Soldiers' Barracks**.

THE FAR NORTH

Located to the north of Gros Islet, **Cap Estate** ❼ lies in hilly land that was once heavily forested. Crops such as tobacco thrived here before the sugar boom of the 18th and 19th centuries resulted in the land being cleared to plant sugar cane. The properties that sit on the former 607-hectare (1,500-acre)

ART DETOUR

In a mansion house on Cap Estate is **Llewellyn Xavier's Studio** (tel: 758-450 9155; www.llewellynxavier.com), where the work of the St Lucian multi-media artist can be viewed only by appointment. His art is exhibited in the permanent collections of museums and galleries all over the world including the Smithsonian Institution in Washington, the Metropolitan Museum of Art and the Museum of Art in New York and the National Gallery in Jamaica. Xavier's work can also be seen at the Caribbean Art Gallery (tel: 758-452 8071), at Rodney Bay Marina.

The artist's use of oils, watercolours and mixed media reflect the vibrant colours and rich textures of the Caribbean. The artwork *Environmental Fragile*, which was created from cardboard and other recycled material, was commemorated in a postage stamp issue in 2006.

Xavier's first major work in the 1970s was a series of 25 prints dedicated to George Jackson, a young man whose incarceration in America became an international cause célèbre.

plantation today are the exclusive homes of the wealthy and luxury rental villas. Residents and guests from the nearby hotels can take advantage of the golf course at the **St Lucia Golf & Country Club** (tel: 758-450 8523; www.stluciagolf. com), which has a pro shop and club rental.

The far north of St Lucia is the driest part of the island and much of the coast is rocky and rough where the waters of the Caribbean Sea meet the Atlantic Ocean in the St Lucia Channel. There are, however, a couple of pleasant beaches on the northwestern coast, which have inevitably attracted hotel development. The picturesque Bécune Point and the golden sand beach of **Anse Bécune** form the northern edge of Cap Estate. The beach is dominated by a large, all-inclusive hotel, Smugglers Cove, but there is public access to the beach and sea.

The owner of a Cas En Bas beach bar

A little further north, there is excellent snorkelling to be had at **Smuggler's Cove**. With a sheltered beach and rugged cliff landscape, it is often a little quieter than Anse Bécune. Cap Maison Hotel maintains a beach bar here with water sports for guests.

Beyond this is **Cariblue Bay**, a pretty, golden sand beach, which is home to LeSport, another all-inclusive resort.

At the far north tip of St Lucia is **Pointe du Cap**. At a little under 150m (470ft) high, in a hilly region beyond the Saline Point residential development, Pointe du Cap provides panoramic views across the north coast to Martinique, west to the Caribbean Sea and east to the Atlantic Ocean. The sea below the sheer cliffs is rough and the land is dry scrub with cacti a common sight. To the east is **Pointe Hardy** where paths for walkers criss-cross

Kite-surfing

the undulating land. The area around Pointe Hardy and north of Cas-en-Bas is part of the large St Lucia Golf and Country Club development.

There are no beaches that can offer safe swimming on this rough, wild and windy Atlantic part of the coast.

South of Pointe Hardy on the northeast Atlantic side of the island is **Cas-en-Bas** ❽, known for its collection of quiet beaches. There are no lifeguards, not all the beaches are well maintained and the roads leading to this coast are rough and hard to negotiate, but they are ideal if you want a quiet day away from it all.

To get to Cas-en-Bas, take the road across the golf course, which winds its way to the luxury villa resort, Cotton Bay. The road ends here, blocked by private land for development, and you have to continue on foot down the track to the sea. Alternatively, take the Cas-en-Bas Road from Gros Islet. The beaches are in a sheltered and rocky bay and, although the Atlantic waters can be rough, the swimming and snorkelling are usually good. There is a laid-back beach bar, with sun loungers outside and kite-surfing available. Horses on the beach make the sand dirty, but it is pleasant to walk along the rocky coastline.

EAST OF CASTRIES

East of Castries is the north's picturesque rural interior that stretches across to the rugged Atlantic coast. The land is largely given over to agriculture and small village communities. If you are starting from Rodney Bay, turn off the Castries–Gros Islet Highway north of Choc Bay and the Bois d'Orange district. The Allan Bousquet Highway leads to the village of Monchy, Babonneau, Fond Assau and Desbarra.

Rain Forest Adventures ziplining

South of Monchy, through winding roads, is **Babonneau** in the heart of farmland and plantations. The area around Babonneau and Fond Assau is thought to be the place to which the last group of African-born enslaved people were transported, which probably accounts for the strong African tradition that has been retained.

Fond Latisab Creole Park ❾ (Sun–Fri, tours by appointment; tel: 758-450 5461) is a few miles south east of Babonneau via narrow country lanes in the small farming community of Fond Assau. The 4-hectare (11-acre) working farm cultivates nutmeg, cocoa and cinnamon and produces its own honey. Fond Latisab maintains many aspects of traditional St Lucian culture, some of which stem back to when Amerindians

Crayfish

A traditional crayfish pot is made of strips of bamboo lashed together, forming a tube that is laid on the river bed. One end is sealed while the other has a flap to allow access to the creatures caught in the pot. Bait can include fresh coconut.

inhabited the land, and practises farm techniques that have been passed on from father to son. For example, local guides are summoned by drumbeat. Even though there is a phone on the farm, much communication is done using the ancient art of drumming. Visitors can watch log sawing done to the beating of drums accompanied by a *chak chak* band (named after the sound made by a local instrument). Log sawing by traditional method requires two men with skill rather than brute force to work the 3kg (6lb) tool. While sawing, the men sing Kwéyòl folk songs, accompanied by the band and the drum beats, which help to maintain rhythm. You can also see local people crayfishing, using traditional bamboo pots, and making cassava bread and farine – a flour produced from cassava grown on the estate. Cassava bread is on sale when there is a tour, and home-grown nutmeg and cinnamon can also be purchased.

Down the road from Fond Latisab, in Chassin, at the foot of La Sorcière hill, is the popular **Rain Forest Adventures** ⑩ (Dec–May Tue–Sun; entrance fee; tel: 758-458 5151; www. rainforestadventure.com). During a 2-hour tour, visitors are transported high above the forest in an aerial tram, which provides a bird's eye view of the landscape. Each gondola

Waves crash at Grand Anse Bay

carries eight seated people and a guide to point out the different plants and trees as you glide through the forest canopy. After the ride you can buckle up to zip line through the forest, an adrenaline rush which is hugely enjoyable and great fun, with only basic levels of fitness and health required. You can also take a guided nature walk. The Jacquot Trail up **Mount La Sorcière** starts from here, and guides are available for birdwatching hikes up the mountain at sunrise to try to spot the St Lucia parrot, which few visitors see in the wild.

Northwest of Babonneau, the winding Allan Bousquet Highway follows the Choc River, eventually leading to the **Union Nature Trail ⑪** (daily 9am–4pm; no guided tours at the weekend; entrance fee) on an outpost of the Forestry and Lands Department. The trail loop begins on a path near the ranger station and can be covered in about an hour. It is a short walk (1.6km/1 mile) through dry forest with a few small hills, and can be enjoyed by any relatively fit visitor.

The collection of wildlife on the property is small, but includes native species such as agouti, iguana and the St Lucia parrot. There is also a herb garden growing plants with medicinal properties, that are used as traditional cures.

GRAND ANSE

East of **Desbarra** stretches the beautiful beach at **Grande Anse ⑫**, best known as a seasonal nesting site for the endangered leatherback turtle (*Demochelys coriacea*) as well as the hawksbill and green turtles. The village of Desbarra is perched on top of a mountain. The paved road stops here and a 4WD is essential unless you want a very long walk downhill. The beach can be seen in the distance just after the track passes the football field.

The secluded 2km (1.2-mile) strip of sand has reportedly been the target of illegal sand-miners. There have also been attempts to take valuable nesting turtles and their eggs. From March to August the beach is monitored by the **Desbarra Grande Anse Turtle Watch Programme**, a community group that works in conjunction with the Ministry of Agriculture, Forestry and Fisheries.

There are organised guided patrols of the beach to monitor the turtles and their nests during the nesting season. The turtle watch patrols begin in the early evening and continue until the following morning. The tours, which are part of the **St Lucia Heritage Tourism Programme** (HERITAS; tel: 758-458 1454; www.heritage

Marigot Bay's greenery

Yachts at anchor beyond the small coconut palm tree-lined beach of the Marigot Beach Club

toursstlucia.org), are led by guides from the local community and welcome visitors from home and abroad.

The beach lies at the edge of the Grande Anse Estate, formerly a vast plantation spanning 810 hectares (2,000 acres). Today, much of the estate lands are uncultivated with cacti and dry forest peppering the hills and cliffs, providing a habitat for rare birds that include the St Lucia wren, the St Lucia oriole and the white-breasted thrasher. Snakes, such as the poisonous fer-de-lance and boa constrictor, and the protected iguana also form part of the estate's endemic wildlife.

MARIGOT BAY AND ROSEAU VALLEY

South of Castries, the verdant St Lucian countryside opens up with wide expanses of farmland bordered by dense forest and laced by rivers. The Millennium Highway leads south out of Castries and towards the West Coast Road.

Within minutes, the beginning of the semi-industrial area of the **Cul de Sac Valley** appears. At the side of the highway is a green space known as the Millennium Park, used as an open-air venue for a variety of festivities including New Year celebrations. In **Grande Cul de Sac Bay** beyond the park is a natural deep harbour and a large terminal and storage facility for Hess Oil.

ROSEAU VALLEY

At the end of the Millennium Highway the West Coast Road starts to climb past the Lucelec power station, which provides the main electricity supply to the greater part of the island. A little further on is the small village of La Croix on the edge of the rainforest. From this village, plantation land stretches away into the distance – this is the **Roseau Valley**. The sprawling Roseau Plantation once extended over both the Roseau and the Cul de Sac valleys.

MARIGOT BAY

The picturesque harbour of **Marigot Bay** ⑬ is off the West Coast Road. There is a small palm-fringed beach and a sheltered natural harbour, which includes a yacht and sailing base, making the bay a popular choice among local sailors and visitors who spend the winter in the Caribbean. On the south side of the bay is a luxury resort and marina, which can accommodate the mega-yachts of the wealthy. The north side of the bay is accessible only by boat, but that small detail doesn't appear to put people off: Marigot Bay is well known for its lively nightlife. As the evening descends the traffic across the bay increases with boats sailing to-and-fro. An inexpensive and regular ferry (water taxi) service operates 24 hours per day. The water around the Marigot Beach Club Hotel and Dive Resort is ideal for swimming and the resort also fronts the area's best beach. The hotel's restaurant, Dolittle's, is named after the film that was shot here in the 1960s.

The eastern part of the lagoon has a small mangrove swamp, a natural site

Talk to the animals

Marigot Bay was immortalised on the silver screen when it was used as a location for the 1967 Hollywood film, *Dr Dolittle*, starring Rex Harrison.

that has been protected with reserve status. A boardwalk runs through the mangrove linking the dock where the water taxis are to the St Lucian-owned and operated JJ's Paradise Resort.

At the heart of the Roseau Valley plantation area is the small village of **Roseau** which stands near farmland once owned by Geest before it was broken up and taken over by individual farmers. Today many of the farms form part of an agricultural collective providing bananas for European supermarkets. This is one of St Lucia's main banana producing regions and contains the largest banana plantation on the island.

RUM DISTILLERY

Cane sugar production fuelled the rum industry on the island but by the 1970s sugar cane was no longer being

SUGAR CANE

Before bananas, sugar was the agricultural mainstay and it is this crop that transformed the lush river valleys in the 18th century. The demand for sugar and its by-products, especially rum, from Europe and further afield prompted St Lucian farmers to import enslaved men and women from West Africa to carry out the back-breaking work on the land until slavery was abolished in the 19th century.

Successful for a time, St Lucia was forced to diversify in the mid-20th century following the introduction to Europe of cheaper sugar produced from sugar beet and fierce competition from high-volume sugar producers elsewhere in the Caribbean. The Roseau sugar refinery struggled on but eventually it too gave up; it was one of the last sugar factories to close in 1963.

Anse La Raye village

grown here. The Barnard family estate, which operated a distillery in Dennery, entered into a joint venture with Geest and moved to the Roseau Valley. Molasses, the raw material for rum production, are now shipped in from Guyana and today the **St Lucia Distillers** (Mon–Fri 9am–3pm; entrance fee; reservations essential 24 hrs in advance, call for tour times; tel: 758-456 3148; www.saintluciarums.com) produces a wide selection of rums and liqueurs. Among the dark rums, look for the award-winning Admiral Rodney, an aged rum which should be drunk neat, or the Chairman's Reserve, also good on the rocks. Bounty is the dark rum you will see most commonly on the island, while Crystal is the white rum used in cocktails.

The distillery is signposted from the West Coast Road. Travelling from north to south, pass the Marigot Bay turn and Marigot school, and continue until you reach a junction. Take a right along a rough, pot-holed access road (muddy in the rain).

Friday fish fry in Anse La Raye

At the end is the rum factory, with a visitors' centre, a shop and a warehouse. This was also the site of a 19th-century, steam-powered sugar mill, with a narrow-gauge railway and steam engine used to transport the cane and molasses. The distillery organises lively guided tours, which reveal how rum was made in the past and how it is produced today. The tour ends with a rum buffet where you can try the 20 or so products they make, from sweet flavoured rums (peanut, coconut, cocoa) to the Denros 160° proof firewater.

ANSE LA RAYE

The West Coast Road weaves through the historically important village of Massacré and descends to sleepy **Anse La Raye ⑮**. At first glance there isn't much to recommend the village; its narrow streets are lined with nondescript small shops and residences. Along the sea front small, brightly painted fishing boats bob in the water and fishermen's huts on the beach provide shelter and shade for repairing a seine (net). The pace is relaxed and as people go about their business visitors can get a sense of the real St Lucia without the tourist gloss.

Friday evening is a different story altogether, for this is when the village wakes up and comes alive with a **Friday fish fry**. In the early evening the road is blocked off as stallholders set up coal pots and barbecues in front of the fishermen's huts and lay out tables so that people can enjoy their meal in the open air while they soak up the atmosphere. By 9pm the place is packed and loud music punctuates the air while locals and visitors alike walk the length of the road to see what's on offer. On sale are fish most likely caught that day, such as red snapper, kingfish and dolphin (dorado or mahi-mahi), and lobster when in season, along with potfish, conch salad, breadfruit salad and floats and bakes (similar to fried dumplings), washed down with a Piton beer or soft drink. The village bars are also busy with the usual end-of-the-week crowd swelled by people at the fish fry. Some very basic public facilities are available near the fishermen's huts.

SOUFRIÈRE AND THE SOUTHWEST COAST

Though tiny, even by Caribbean standards, the island encompasses a wide variety of landscapes from open plains to rolling hills and valleys, ragged mountain ranges and lush rainforest. In places you can see that the road has been literally cut through the hills and is shaded by mature

Religious art

The small hill community of **Jacmel**, which lies east of the Roseau Valley, has a church with a striking painting of a black Madonna and child and other St Lucian figures by the artist Dunstan St Omer. It is best visited with a local guide, as even in daylight the winding, narrow roads are difficult to negotiate.

*The famous twin Piton mountain
peaks, from Soufrière beach*

trees and vegetation, while farms and fishing villages dot the panorama below. The journey from Castries to Soufrière takes about an hour and a quarter, even though the distance between the two places is only about 32km (20 miles). You must have your wits about you if you intend to drive yourself because these winding mountain roads can be unforgiving, with steep drops down to the valley below and often mudslides after heavy rain. In places there are stunning views of the coast and the Pitons – Gros Piton and Petit Piton – as the road skirts along the cliffs.

Where the road widens in a curve in the road, opposite a stand of trees at **Anse La Verdure**, is **Plas Kassav** ⑯ (daily 8.30am–7 or 8pm; tel: 758-459 4050; www.plaskassavinc. com). This family bakery uses traditional methods and some innovative equipment to produce farine (from cassava) and a mouth-watering variety of (gluten-free) cassava bread that is popular with local workers, especially at lunchtime. Several cruise ships and organised tours make this a regular stop, providing people with an opportunity to taste one of the island's specialities. Attached to the bakery is a small shop that sells refreshments and cassava bread in a choice of flavours including coconut, peanut butter, cherry and raisin, cinnamon, salt, saltfish and smoked herring. The bread makes a hearty snack or can be used as an accompaniment to a meal. Other local products such as dried bananas, pepper sauces and honey are also sold in the shop.

A few minutes drive from Anse La Verdure is **Canaries** (pronounced can-ar-ees), a small village where most families eke out a living from the fruits of the sea. The name originates from an Amerindian pot (called a *kannawi*) used by the people who settled here. The **Canaries River** flows through the forest and out to sea here, supporting a handful of waterfalls to the south of the village. Most are hard to find without a guide and require a 30-minute hike, at the very least, to reach them.

A few minutes south of Canaries, off the West Coast Road is **Anse La Liberté**. The land, which is managed by the St Lucia National Trust, extends 56 hectares (138 acres) into the forest. It has around 6km (4 miles) of walking trails, a good beach and some basic visitor facilities. You can also reach it by water taxi from Canaries. Anse La Liberté is thought to have historical significance. It is believed that enslaved African men and women living and working on the island celebrated their emancipation here in 1834, hence the name – Anse La Liberté (Bay of Freedom).

As the road snakes through the hills you can enjoy stunning views of the sea and the spectacular western landscape backed by the magnificent Pitons, which dominate the area,

HURRICANE TOMAS

The hilly terrain of the west coast of St Lucia means it is particularly susceptible to mudslides caused by torrential rain, which often lead to fatalities and huge farming losses. In 2010, landslides caused by rain associated with Hurricane Tomas killed 14 people.

lying just beyond the centre of Soufrière. Before that, **Mount Tabac** comes into view, rising high above the hills and forests to its 678m (2,224ft) peak.

SOUFRIÈRE

For many years after the country was ceded to the British, **Soufrière** ⓱ remained little more than a small fishing village, but today it is expanding. The population of the village proper and its environs is now believed to be close to

MARINE PROTECTION

The **Soufrière Marine Management Area** (SMMA), extending from Anse Jambon to Anse L'Ivrogne almost at the foot of Gros Piton, protects the unique marine habitat along the west coast of St Lucia, monitors the coral reefs and water quality, and carryies out scientific research in an attempt to prevent damage to reefs, fish stock, beaches and vegetation.

Its four main protected Marine Reserve Areas (MRAs), for which you will require a permit to dive, are: Anse Chastanet, Rachette Pointe, Petit Piton, Gros Piton (restricted access). Permits can be purchased on an annual or daily basis and are available from the SMMA (tel: 758-459 5500) and authorised dive operators.

To protect the reefs:

Do not damage or touch the coral while you are snorkelling or diving.

Do not remove any plants, animals, fish or even shells from the sea.

Do not feed the fish.

Tie up only to mooring buoys or anchor at official sandy areas.

Do not buy souvenirs made from coral; it is illegal to remove it from St Lucia.

Do not buy souvenirs or other items made from turtle shells.

Do not litter; dispose of waste in the appropriate bins.

8,000. Soufrière can be eas-
ily explored on foot; there
are few sights, and most are
within a few minutes' walk of
the water. Most of the area's
attractions are either on, or
underneath the water, or in
and around the rainforest.
To the east is **Mount Gimie**,
which at more than 950m
(3,145ft) high stands above
both of the better-known
peaks of the Pitons.

Colourful Soufrière rooftops

Soufrière is St Lucia's oldest town and was the capital when
France controlled the island. It stands in the shadow of the
island's most striking and best-known landmark – the twin
peaks of the Pitons rising majestically out of the sea. Louis XIV
of France granted around 809 hectares (2,000 acres) of land
to the Devaux family, who ran a successful plantation growing
sugar, cocoa, tobacco and cotton on the estate. Descendants of
the family still own land and property in the area today.

Enter the village via a small bridge over the **Soufrière
River**, which flows to the sea just to the west. On the left is
a petrol station, to the right is the town hall and after that,
business and residential properties line both sides of Bridge
Street, the main road. Modern and colonial buildings stand
side by side; painted in pastels, many have pretty balconies with gingerbread fretwork. Most notable is the **Old
Courthouse** constructed of stone in 1898 at the southern end
of the waterfront.

The waterfront has a small paved area with seats looking
out across the harbour, which is often dominated by the sail-
assisted cruise ships that frequent the port for a few hours.

Mooring up at Anse Chastanet beach

The deep harbour drops to 60m (200ft) close to shore so large yachts can dock right at the pier.

At the northern end of the pier is another jetty, the **Soufrière Marine Management Area** (SMMA) office, a water taxi station and tour office where you can book transport around the coast. Visitors can go to places that are difficult to reach by road, and also to some of the island's best dive sites, as well as join boat trips around the Pitons.

The airy **Lady of Assumption Church**, built in the 1950s, stands at the corners of Henry Belmar, Sir Arthur Lewis and Boulevard streets. It has a simple design with the lovely altar and pulpit made from dark tropical wood. Above the main doors is a magnificent pipe organ.

Just in front of the church steps is the **town square** where a guillotine was erected by the Brigands (see page 19) during the French Revolution. If you wander through the small square be aware that this is one place where there is relatively high unemployment. You may be solicited for money or be approached by an unofficial (and unwanted) guide offering to show you around the church; a guide is not necessary, so a firm but polite refusal should suffice. On the north side of the square, on Henry Belmar Street, you will find buses for

Castries and on the south side, on Sir Arthur Lewis Street, are buses for Vieux Fort and the south.

ANSE CHASTANET

Anse Chastanet ⑱ is a national marine park and well-known dive area just north of Soufrière, but the access road is pot-holed and narrow so you would be best advised to take a water taxi around the bay. The Anse Chastanet Resort and its sister property, Jade Mountain, dominate the beaches and 243 hectares (600 acres) of verdant hillside here. Spacious and luxurious tree-house style, open-air rooms built in to the hillside look out to the Pitons, and a dive operation, **Scuba St Lucia**, rents snorkelling and scuba-diving equipment. PADI and NAUI scuba courses are available for everyone, from beginners to the more experienced.

Volcanic black sand fronts the hotel, while the **Anse Chastanet reef**, with a host of colourful marine life, offers the opportunity to walk to a dive site within a few metres of the shore, where there are bright displays of coral, sponges, angelfish, parrot fish and seahorses. North of Anse Chastanet are two fine golden sand beaches, **Anse Mamin and Anse Jambon**. Anse Mamin is ideal for a picnic or a day spent relaxing on the beach and its clear waters. The beach is backed by forest and former plantation land from where **Bike St Lucia** (tel: 758-459 2453; www.bike stlucia.com) organises ener-getic cycling trips, known as

Join a Bike St Lucia tour to experience jungle-biking

jungle biking, along 19km (12 miles) of bike trails through the 18th-century plantation.

DIAMOND BOTANICAL GARDENS

South of Soufrière, old estate houses and hotels populate the hillsides, mostly shielded from the road by magnificent trees and bordered by fertile farmland. Head east out of town on Sir Arthur Lewis Street and a few kilometres along a good road you will reach the **Diamond Botanical Gardens, Mineral Baths and Waterfall** ⑲ (Mon–Sat 10am–5pm, Sun and public hols 10am–3pm; entrance fee; tel: 758-459 7565; www.diamondstlucia.com). The gardens were originally part of the Soufrière Estate, awarded to the Devaux family in the early 18th century by King Louis XIV of France. The original baths were built in 1784 by the Governor of St Lucia, Baron

The spectacular Diamond waterfall

de Laborie, after it was discovered that water from the sulphur springs was mineral rich and therefore an effective treatment for rheumatism and other ailments. The baths were financed by King Louis XVI for his troops on the island, but they were destroyed during battles with the Brigands around the time of the French Revolution. The bathing pools were restored in 1925, while the garden and other facilities were expanded later to provide

Morne Coubaril Estate

bathing in a communal outdoor pool or individual baths, for an additional fee. Beyond the baths is the waterfall.

A short trail snakes through the gardens and useful and descriptive signs identify tropical flora such as fragrant frangipani, red ginger, vibrant hibiscus and a variety of trees laden with coconut, cocoa or other local staples, so a guide is not necessary. A longer and more strenuous hike, which crosses over the **Diamond River**, leads to the old mill and a working waterwheel.

MORNE COUBARIL ESTATE

Morne Coubaril Estate [20] (daily 9am–4pm; entrance fee; guided tours; tel: 758-459 7340; www.stluciaziplining.com) lies less than 1km (0.6 mile) from Soufrière on the Soufrière–Vieux Fort Road, almost opposite the slip road leading to the Sugar Beach (also known as Jalousie Plantation) resort. The 113-hectare (280-acre) working plantation is one of the oldest on the island. It was owned by the Devaux family until 1960 when it was taken over by Donald Monplaisir. The Monplaisir family have attempted to restore and preserve the property and its agricultural traditions. The great house with lovely wrap-around verandas is not open to the public because it remains a family home.

Colourful flora and trees heavy with fruit such as papaya, banana, cocoa, coconut, orange and grapefruit grow in abundance. At the Copra House, coconuts are prepared for sale to the St Lucia Coconut Growers Association, which produces coconut oil, and there is a lovely view over the deep bay nearby. You can also see a fully operational sugar mill where a mule is used to turn the wheel that grinds the sugar cane and produces the juice to make sugar and rum.

Replica wooden slave quarters reveal how people were forced to live in basic and cramped conditions. The huts have

AMERINDIAN HERITAGE

The area around Soufrière has been an important settlement for centuries, long before the French or British arrived. The Amerindian settlers were in awe of the volcano, where the Island Arawaks thought their god, Yokahu, slept and the Kalinago (Caribs) named it Qualibou, or the place of death. Archaeological evidence of their presence can still be found on the ground.

There are petroglyphs along paths on both the **Jalousie** and **Stonefield Estates**. The former Jalousie Plantation hotel (now Sugar Beach) was built amid a wave of controversy when local people, environmentalists and archaeologists objected to its location due to its proximity to the Pitons, now a UNESCO World Heritage Site, and also because it was built on an important Amerindian burial ground, which is now under the tennis courts.

been reconstructed using traditional methods, with mud and paper on the walls and palm thatch on the roof.

An added extra is the opportunity to experience the adrenaline rush of zip-lining in full view of Petit Piton along eight zip lines through the estate and a canopy of fruit trees. Morne Coubaril also organises trekking expeditions on horseback (by appointment) and a choice of rainforest hikes (up to 3 hours) that visit the **Coubaril**

La Soufrière Sulphur Springs

waterfall, which is fed by the Sulphur Springs. Though strenuous, the walks are fun with an informative guide and reach a lookout point that provides a panoramic view over Soufrière.

SULPHUR SPRINGS PARK

Off the Soufrière–Vieux Fort Road are **La Soufrière Sulphur Springs** ㉑ (daily 9am–5pm; entrance fee), notable for the pungent odour (hydrogen sulphide), not dissimilar to rotten eggs. The Park contains the most active and hottest geothermal area in the Lesser Antilles and there are plans for the energy to be harnessed to produce electricity.

La Soufrière volcano collapsed more than 40,000 years ago and now produces only the foul-smelling gases and hot water that can reach temperatures of 170°C (338°F), but it is known as a 'drive-in' volcano. The rocky landscape of the geothermal field looks like something from a science-fiction movie, with springs and grey-brown mud bubbling up sporadically.

At the ticket booth, be prepared for vendors who congregate here to offer their wares; official guides also wait to escort visitors, for an additional fee, down a wooden pathway and along some uneven ground. He or she will give you a rundown of the site and its history. Tour operators offer a package of a visit to the springs, a mud bath and natural spa in a warm waterfall. The concrete bath can get very crowded when a tour party is in, so it is best to go early. Be aware that the mud will stain your clothes.

RABOT ESTATE

At the turn off for the volcano is the entrance for the **Rabot Estate** ㉒ (tel: 758-457 1624; www.thehotelchocolat.com), a recently rehabilitated 56-hectare (140-acre) cocoa plantation owned by the British chocolatiers, Hotel Chocolat. The plantation dates back to 1745 and is the oldest on the island, with some very rare old trees of scientific and chocolate interest. This is a true bean-to-bar experience, as they grow their own cocoa before making it into their own delicious St Lucia chocolate in the UK. Local cocoa farmers also benefit as the estate buys their quality cacao pods at premium prices and guarantees a market for their product while also supplying them with young trees to improve their stock.

Ripe cocoa pods

In 2012, a hotel was opened on the estate with luxury cottages and villas in view of the Pitons, together with the Boucan restaurant which specializes in all things chocolate, both savoury and sweet [see page 113]. You can walk to the site of the 1795 Battle of Rabot, stroll through the plantation tasting the fruits of the mango, guava, soursop and papaya trees, then relax with a cocoa massage using the cacao nibs, oil and butter.

FOND DOUX ESTATE

South of Rabot Estate is the **Fond Doux Estate** ㉓ (daily 8am–4pm for tours, until 10pm for dinner; entrance fee; tel: 758-459 7545; www.fonddouxestate.com], a working plantation. An inexpensive guided tour includes a look at the original plantation house, built in 1864

A cocoa farmer polishes the beans at Fondoux Plantation

and renovated in the 1990s, which is currently occupied. Adjacent to the estate house is a colonial-style restaurant, which serves a buffet lunch for tour groups, a bar and a souvenir shop. The grounds, which extend over 55 hectares (135 acres), are planted with coffee, banana, mango, citrus fruits and coconut. Surplus spices, fruit and vegetables are sold in the owners' supermarket in Soufrière. There is still an original worker's house, store house, copra house and coffee-drying area on the property, as well as cottages available to rent.

Cocoa grown here is shipped to the UK and to the United States for use in chocolate produced by the Hershey Food Corporation. The drying racks are still in operation and you

A guide swinging from vines in the Edmund Forest Reserve

will be shown how cocoa sticks are made. These are available to buy in the shop. A leisurely walk through the estate reveals an abundance of bright and fragrant flora such as heliconia, ginger lilies and anthuriums. Trails through the estate lead past ruined military buildings built by French engineers in the 18th century, while up on the hill is an old Brigands' hideout.

RAINFOREST MOUNTAIN RESERVES

Most of the mountainous heart of St Lucia has been declared forest reserve, partly to protect wildlife and partly to preserve water supply for the settlements around the coast of the island. In some areas there are trails through the forest, maintained by the Forestry Department (tours Mon–Fri 8.30am–3pm; entrance fee; tel: 758-468 5649 or 450 2231; http://malff.com; see page 90), and it is possible to hike from west to east coasts starting from Soufrière.

A simple walk in the rainforest is a rewarding experience, preferably with a Forest Ranger to guide you. Six miles (10km) east of Soufrière lies the village of **Fond St Jacques**, where there are paintings by Dunstan St Omer in the church. From the village, there is a poor road leading up to a Rangers' station. To reach it, either use a four-wheel drive vehicle or walk.

With advance notice, the rangers will escort you through the **Edmund Forest Reserve** to the **Quilesse Forest Reserve** and down to the Rangers' station on the **Des Cartiers Rainforest Trail**, near Mahaut and to Micoud on the east coast. Alternatively, for a shorter excursion, follow the **Enbas Saut Trail 24** from the Rangers' station above Fond St Jacques. This steep but exhilarating trail winds down 2,112 steps cut in the hillside to the Troumassée River, providing an opportunity to see elfin woodland, cloud forest and rainforest, depending on your altitude. You will be able to see the peaks of Piton Canarie, Piton Troumassée and Morne Gimie and you will hear the St Lucian parrot in the trees above you. At the bottom there are a couple of river crossings before you reach a pool with a little waterfall, where you can cool off before the arduous hike back up. Expect to get wet and muddy, especially after rain, which is frequent.

A hiker at the summit of Grande Piton

THE PITONS

The Pitons dominate the southwestern landscape around Soufrière. **Petit Piton** (743m/2,438ft) is to the north of Soufrière harbour, while **Gros Piton** (798m/2,618ft) is on the south side of the bay near the L'Ivrogne River. The tall volcanic cones, which are covered in rich vegetation, are undoubtedly the most photographed rocks in

Petit Piton peak

St Lucia. A UNESCO World Heritage Site, their image appears on everything from postcards to T-shirts and art.

For many people the Pitons offer pleasure simply for their sheer beauty. However, more adventurous spirits want to get to the top. Though Petit Piton is the smaller of the two, it is more difficult to climb because of its steep sides, making climbing ropes essential. A relatively easier option is the trail up Gros Piton, although this isn't a walk in the park either. It is not a pursuit to be tackled alone and you will need to employ the services of a local guide. Contact the Soufrière Regional Development Foundation (tel: 758-459 5500; http://soufrierefoundation.org), or the Gros Piton Guides Association (Fond Gens Libre Interpretative Centre, 40 mins from Soufrière, tel: 758-459 3492; open daily 8am-3pm). Be prepared for a very early start – most guides recommend setting off and reaching your goal early in the morning before it gets too hot.

Scaling the peak can be hot and thirsty work, so remember to carry plenty of water, sunblock and a hat. The time taken to complete the climb can vary; it is generally between three and six hours each way depending on the hiker's level of fitness. From the summit you will be rewarded with sweeping panoramic views over the island, north and south, and on a clear day as far as neighbours Martinique and St Vincent.

The **Tet Paul Trail** is an easy alternative for those not fit enough to scale Gros Piton. This 45-minute walk begins in the **Chateau Belair** community in 2.4 hectares (6 acres) of lush vegetation between Fond Doux and the Gros Piton Trail. Head for Fond Doux and you will see the sign at the entrance to the Plantation. You walk through a variety of fruit trees and medicinal plants and can enjoy views of the Pitons, Jalousie beach, the coastline to the south and the neighbouring islands.

VIEUX FORT AND THE SOUTH

The road south from Soufrière to Vieux Fort dips and rises through the hills and valleys, skirting forest and farmland, eventually passing the small fishing hamlets that dot the southwestern coast. It takes less than an hour to reach Vieux Fort.

CHOISEUL

Choiseul is a good-size town with a developed centre that has a town hall, a church, several schools, a post office and petrol station. The ruins of **Fort Citreon**, a fortress which protected Choiseul Bay, still stands guard over the area, but Choiseul is best known for **La Fargue Craft Centre** ㉕ (tel: 758-454 3226), south of the village. This is where local artisans sell their work, such as clay

A bedroom seen through shuttered windows at Balenbouche Estate

pots, for which the area is well known, basketwork, wood-carvings, local spices, seasonings and sauces. The centre is on the main road and has plenty of parking space. The centre can direct you to craftsmen's workshops if you want something a bit different which is not in stock.

BALENBOUCHE ESTATE

A few miles down the road is the **Balenbouche Estate** ㉖ (daily; entrance fee; guided tours by appointment; tel: 758-455 1244; www.balenbouche.com), which stands proudly on 30 hectares (75 acres) between the Balenbouche and Piaye rivers. It is close to some important historical and archaeological sites, and nearby **Morne le Blanc** has a good lookout point. The first European settlement at Balenbouche was established in the mid-18th century.

White sand on Anse de Sables beach

Today, the great house stands on the site of two previous estate houses. It dates from the mid-19th century and is furnished with antiques from that period. There are cottages to rent, a restaurant, nature trail and pretty gardens as well as ruins such as the slave quarters and the old plantation's sugar mill and water wheel with mechanical works that were shipped from England.

In the beginning

Hewanorra International Airport is named after an Amerindian word meaning 'land of the iguana'. There have been significant archaeological finds in the south of the island, where the airport is located.

There have been several significant archaeological discoveries made on the estate, including pre-Columbian petroglyphs, ceramics and stone tools.

Two dark-sand, rough beaches are **Balenbouche Bay**, just a five-minute walk through the estate, and **Anse Touloulu**, a ten-minute walk.

LABORIE

The journey continues southeast skirting round and above **Laborie** ㉗, a small fishing community with wooden colonial buildings in its centre and some modern fishing huts on the edge of the water. The village also has the best beach in the area, pretty but quiet, populated by a handful of local fishermen. Laborie has a small selection of accommodation for visitors who prefer to stay away from the crowds and several good local restaurants.

VIEUX FORT

Vieux Fort ㉘, considered to be St Lucia's second city, is one of the oldest settlements at St Lucia's most southerly tip 67km (42 miles) from Castries, with a developing industrial

Cap Moule à Chique's lighthouse

centre and a population of 15,000. **Hewanorra International Airport** is located here, on the plains that open out to the sea. There are a few hotels, mainly B&Bs, not far from the airport, and some developed industry around the large port area, such as oilstorage, warehouses and grain stores, and a wharf lined with shipping containers. Here, too, is one of the Eastern Caribbean's commercial free-zone centres and a large fisheries complex, along with a busy, if slightly haphazard, shopping area. Modern villas rub shoulders with fading French colonial-style buildings, reflecting the historical origins of the town's first French settlers. The older part of town is full of small grocery stores, typical Caribbean shops, takeaways and bakeries.

Anse de Sables is a beautiful strip of white-sand beach on the east coast of the island. The waters just offshore are popular with windsurfers and kitesurfers who come to take advantage of the trade winds that bless this coast. There is a little bar and restaurant and a surf centre, where boards and equipment can be rented. A little further north is an all-inclusive resort.

CAP MOULE À CHIQUE

Cap Moule à Chique ㉙ is a rocky outcrop with dry forest and a tall lighthouse that towers high above the town and is as far south as you can get on the mainland. The drive up to a lookout is twisting and narrow, bordered by vegetation and sheer cliffs. Several residences dot the winding landscape and the peak.

Standing 223m (730ft) above sea level, the 9m (29ft) **lighthouse** tower is believed to be the second highest in the world, because of its location perched on Cap Moule à Chique. Painted white with a red lantern at the top, the tower itself is closed to the public but the lighthouse site is not. From

PRESERVING THE WHIPTAIL LIZARD

The St Lucia whiptail lizard (*Cnemidophorus vanzoi*) is not only endemic to St Lucia but is the only whiptail found in the Eastern Caribbean. The males sport the colours of the St Lucian flag: black, white, blue and yellow. Cats, rats and mongooses decimated the population until by the 1960s only a few lizards remained on the Maria Islands offshore.

In the 1990s the Forestry Department and the Durrell Wildlife Conservation Trust began a programme to introduce the whiptail to other predator-free offshore islands. A satellite colony on Praslin Island was hugely successful and this was followed in 2008 by introducing whiptails to Rat Island, on the west coast off Castries, in order to widen the gene pool. A further colony on Dennery Island is planned.

Barefoot hiking in the rainforest

this vantage point the view is spectacular: to the north-west, beyond Vieux Fort, are the rolling hills and valleys of southern St Lucia, including the Pitons in the far distance, and **Morne Gomier**, a 313m (1,028ft) -high peak closer to town. To the northeast, just off the coast, you will see the rocky Maria Islands Nature Reserve poking out of the sea like seals. Here, too, are sweeping views up around the East Coast, where the waves of the Atlantic Ocean buffet the land and the rocks below. On a clear day you can see the north coast of St Vincent.

MARIA ISLANDS

Maria Islands Nature Reserve ㉚ (closed during the summer breeding season mid-May to end of July) lies 1.5km (1 mile) east of Vieux Fort, across a narrow ocean channel. The two largest islets, **Maria Major** and **Maria Minor**, form the main part of the nature reserve, which covers 12 hectares (30 acres) of dry scrubland and rocky outcrop.

These compact islands on St Lucia's windward side have been shaped by the rough waves of the Atlantic, and are home to an array of rare bird and plant life. Noddies and terns have protected nesting sites here. Look out for the endemic St Lucia whiptail lizard (*Cnemidophorus vanzoi*) scuttling under bushes (the male has the colours of the national flag), and the non-poisonous kouwess grass snake (*dromicus ornatus*).

Access to the nature reserve is restricted to guided tours run by the St Lucia National Trust Southern Regional Office (tel: 758-454 5014; www.slunatrust.org) (see page 42) and to reach it visitors will need to take a small boat across the channel. Take your swimsuit and snorkelling gear as there is a small beach and plenty of underwater life.

THE EAST COAST

The East Coast Road from Vieux Fort follows a scenic route along the coastline of the windward side of the island. This is the less commercial part of St Lucia with fewer large resorts and hotels than on the west coast, but with a wealth of nature reserves and walking trails through the rainforest, gardens and fishing hamlets.

SAVANNES BAY

North from Vieux Fort is the **Savannes Bay Nature Reserve ㉛**, a protected wetland, the second-largest mangrove swamp in St Lucia, the first being the nearby **Mankoté Mangrove ㉜**, which lies a little further south. An extensive reef system runs from near the Maria Islands (see page 76) to the north end of the Savannes reserve. The protective reef allows for the cultivation of sea moss, which

The freshest fish at Savannes Bay

Discover colourful reefs

is grown on ropes under the water, suspended by hundreds of plastic bottles. A wealth of bird life, such as herons, terns and egrets, inhabit the rich mangrove swamp.

Until the 1960s the Mankoté Mangrove and forest were part of a US military base that stretched across more than 1,200 hectares (3,000 acres). Due to restricted access to the land, the mangrove swamp suffered little or no damage caused by development elsewhere. However, once the US vacated the land, the swamp was opened up to commercial fishermen and hunters, until it was granted reserve status by the government in 1986.

Nearby **Scorpion Island**, lying in the Savannes Bay, also contains red and black mangroves.

Around 16km (9 miles) from Vieux Fort is **Micoud**, a small coastal village and an ideal place to visit during two of the island's biggest religious festivals, La Rose in August and La Marguerite in October. They are both celebrated with church services, street parades, delicious food and fun events.

Inland is the starting and ending point for hikers attempting the walking trail that runs across the island through the Quilesse Forest and Edmund Forest reserves to Fond St Jacques, just outside Soufrière (see page 58). Alternatively, the circular **Des Cartiers Rainforest Trail**, at the start of the route, is about 4km (2.5 miles) and takes 2 hours to complete. There are no steep hills, but the path can be muddy and slippery after rain. Guides at the Rangers' station can escort you. Parrot watching is good here in the early morning, but you must make arrangements with the Forestry Department (tours Mon–Fri 8.30am–3pm; entrance fee; tel: 758-468 5649; http://malff.com) beforehand.

West of Micoud and north of the Troumassée River is **Latille Waterfall** ❸❸ (entrance fee), which has 6m (20ft) cascades that descend into a pool below; bring your swimsuit.

MAMIKU GARDENS

Mamiku Gardens ❸❹ (daily 9am–5pm; entrance fee; tel: 758-455 3729; www.facebook.com/pages/Mamiku-Gardens) has 5 hectares (12 acres) of grounds surrounding an old estate house. It is located off the main road just north of Mon Repos in the Micoud Quarter, not far from Praslin Bay. In the 18th century Mamiku Estate was home to a French governor of the island; it later became a British military outpost during the tussle for ownership. Visitors to the tropical gardens

See water lilies and other plants at Mamiku Gardens

can explore a series of self-guided walking trails lined with orchids, heliconia and hibiscus and shaded by trees, including the gommier, which is still used to make dugout canoes. A small herb garden includes plants used in bush medicine introduced to the island by enslaved West Africans. Also on the site are ruins and archaeological artefacts. There is parking, a snack bar and a gift shop, and the ticket booth has trail maps.

PRASLIN BAY

Praslin Bay ❸❺ is a beautiful deep bay divided into two sections by a small promontory which stretches out like a finger towards the tiny **Praslin Island** offshore. The St Lucian whiptail lizard was introduced here from the Maria Islands in 1995 to conserve the species.

Purple throated carib

In the southern part of the bay, the village of Praslin maintains the fishing tradition on which it grew, and boat builders construct canoes from gommier trees using ancient techniques believed to have been imported by the first Amerindian settlers.

Whiptail lizard

The area's extensive red mangroves and mature trees are the habitat of the harmless endemic boa constrictor, a snake that can grow to over 3.5m (12ft). More than 30 species of bird live here and on the islands, such as the St Lucian oriole, the great white heron and the red-billed tropic bird.

Beyond the mangroves and dry forest is a cave network with evidence of an Amerindian settlement. Petroglyphs and remnants of ceramics and tools have been discovered along these parts.

FREGATE ISLANDS

Just off the coast at the northern perimeter of Praslin Bay is the **Fregate Islands Nature Reserve** ㊱. The two small islands that form the reserve, **Fregate Island Major** and **Fregate Island Minor**, have a combined size of less than 0.5 hectare (1 acre). The islands are named after the frigate bird (*fregata magnificens*), which nests and roosts here, migrating from Cape Verde in Africa, but unfortunately their numbers have dropped dramatically. The islands are covered mostly in xerophytic vegetation, cacti, mangrove forest and grass. The National Trust manages this reserve and Praslin Island, but there are no tours.

Bright houses in Dennery

DENNERY

The East Coast Road soon reaches **Dennery** ㊲, notable for its fishing industry. This is another village with a lively seafood fiesta (Sat 4pm) held on the beachfront with lots of children's activities as well as food, drink and music.

Inland, along the Dennery River, is the **Treetop Adventure Park** ㊳ (Errard Road, daily 10am–4pm; reservations essential; tel: 758-458 0908; www.adventuretoursstlucia.com). Instructors strap you into a harness and you descend the hillside on zip lines through the forest. Also on offer are bike tours along forest trails to the waterfall for bathing, offshore kayaking and a jeep safari, all with knowledgeable guides.

FOND D'OR BAY

About 1.6km (1 mile) from Dennery, where the main road turns west into the Mabouya Valley, is **Fond D'Or Bay**. This crescent-shaped bay has a beach of white sand, backed by sheer cliffs and a rugged landscape. Swimming is not recommended because of the rough sea, but the beach is lovely.

Driving from Dennery, the view of the bay from the roadside lookout point is spectacular. Nearby, an old fort and plantation ruins have been developed as **Fond D'Or Nature Reserve and Historical Park** ㊴ (daily; entrance fee; tel: 758-453 3242), with a wooded canopy of coconut palms, an estuarine forest and mangrove wetlands. Visitors can hike along the forest trails and tour the estate that contains the remnants of the sugar mill, windmill and the old planter's house, which is now an interpretation centre. From one of the trails on the edge of the estate, walkers might spot the hill known locally as **Mabouya** or **La Sorcière** (the sorceress), which stands almost 7km (4 miles) away in the Castries Waterworks Forest Reserve.

TRANSINSULAR ROAD

The road now leaves the coast behind and heads inland and uphill into the forest before climbing over the **Barre de l'Isle**, the ridge which divides the island. At the high point is a stall where Forestry Department guides meet hikers. You can do the short **Barre de l'Isle trail** ④⓪ on your own, or hire a guide for the longer **Mount La Combe** hike. As you emerge from the forest the landscape becomes progressively more built up until the smell from the coffee-roasting factory notifies you that you have arrived on the outskirts of Castries again.

Dennery bay

WHAT TO DO

SPORTS

WATER SPORTS

The west coast of St Lucia is blessed with the warm water of the Caribbean Sea and is the ideal place for a wealth of water sports, with something for all levels of expertise. The east coast, however, is the Atlantic Ocean side of the island and can be lashed by high winds and waves, making most of it unsafe for swimming.

DIVING AND SNORKELLING

Experienced divers can enjoy rich, colourful marine life just a few yards from the beach in some cases, while beginners can take to the water confidently with an expert instructor. The water here is home to angel fish and seahorses, octopus and turtles, colourful coral and spectacular sponges. Several shipwrecks around the coast provide fascinating artificial reefs in addition to the natural reefs.

Some of the island's most beautiful dive sites are located in protected marine areas such as the Soufrière Marine Management Area (SMMA). **Anse Chastanet Reef** attracts novices and experienced divers. The marine life is just a short walk in the water from the volcanic sand beach, and there are caves to explore in the relatively shallow parts.

Many of the larger hotels have dive centres on site, while others can offer dive and accommodation packages with independent operators. **Dive Fair Helen** is a long-established locally-owned operation in Marigot Bay (tel: 758-451 7716, www.divefairhelen.com). **Dive Saint Lucia** (tel: 758-451 3843, www.divesaintlucia.com) has a purpose built training pool and classrooms at Rodney Bay marina. **Scuba St Lucia** is on the

Coconut palm and yachts silhouetted at sunset, Marigot Bay

beach at Anse Chastanet Resort, Soufrière, tel: 758-459 7755, www.scubastlucia.com with the marine park on its doorstep.

Snorkellers of all ages will find schools of colourful fish and other marine life around Anse Mamin, just north of Anse Chastanet and at Anse Cochon, south of Anse La Raye. North and south of Petit Piton, Malgretoute and Beausejour are also excellent spots for snorkelling.

KAYAKING

Explore the island's coast, rivers and shady mangrove swamps by water. Guided kayaking tours can combine birdwatching, historical sites, snorkelling and beaches. **Dive Fair Helen** (Marigot Bay, tel: 758-451 7716, www.dfhkayaking.com) offers a variety of tours, most starting from Marigot Bay, where you can explore the mangroves or Roseau River before heading north to Castries, Rat Island or as far as Pigeon Island, or turning south to Anse Cochon.

Diving over stunning coral

Kayak St Lucia (Anse Chastenet, tel: 758-459 0000; www.kayakstlucia.com) can take you all round the Soufrière area, getting close up and personal with the Pitons, exploring fishing villages and deserted beaches. By private arrangement, you can kayak in the Savannes Bay Nature

Reserve to see the mangroves and hidden coves, but there are no regular tours.

Kayaking

WINDSURFING AND KITESURFING

The southern coast is a magnet for experienced and adventurous windsurfers and kitesurfers who are attracted by the challenge of the strong winds that can whip up the Atlantic waves off Anse de Sables at Vieux Fort.

The best winds blow from December to June, when the trade winds are most consistent and they blow strongly cross-onshore from the left. However, you may still catch a good breeze in the summer months.

Reef Kite and Surf (Anse de Sables Beach, Vieux Fort, tel: 758-454 3418, www.slucia.com/windsurf; www.slucia.com/kitesurf) has plenty of equipment for rent and offers windsurfing and kiteboarding instruction. The centre has good links with several hotels on the island.

Elsewhere, Cas-en-Bas in the northeast is also a popular spot and there are facilities here too offered by **Kitesurfing St Lucia** (Cas-en-Bas, Gros Islet, tel: 758-714 9589, www.kitesurfingstlucia.com).

Less experienced windsurfers may prefer the relatively quiet Caribbean Sea on the west coast. You can rent windsurf boards or kitesurfing equipment, and take lessons at the water sports facilities of the larger hotels and resorts.

FISHING

The warm Caribbean waters are teeming with fish and,

depending on the time of year, you could reel in big game fish such as marlin, wahoo, kingfish, sailfish and dorado (mahi mahi, also known as dolphin); tuna and barracuda can also be caught in these waters. Deep sea or sport fishing is very popular and every year there are numerous events and competitions attended by local and visiting fishermen. Visitors can book an entire day or a half-day fishing trip with companies such as **Captain Mike's** (Vigie Marina, Castries, tel: 758-452 7044, http://captmikes.com) or **Hackshaws Boat Charters** (Vigie Marina, tel: 758-453 0553, www.hackshaws.com).

WHALE-WATCHING

Around this tiny island, many species of resident and migratory whales can be seen in the warm Caribbean Sea. The

Snorkelling over St Lucia's reefs

various species can be seen at different times of year, especially during the migratory mating season from October to April. Most common are sperm whales, pilot whales, humpback whales and false killer whales. Common, spinner, spotted, striped and bottlenose dolphins can also be spotted accompanying the whales, sometimes leaping above the water. The fishing companies above also offer whale watching tours.

A sailing yacht moored up by the coast

SAILING

An exciting way to explore the coast and see the scenic landscape is by boat. Boat tours can include a spot of diving, snorkelling, swimming or sport fishing, and can be day or sunset party cruises. Full- and half-day sails can be arranged through one of the local boat charter companies based at the marinas at Castries, Rodney Bay, Marigot Bay and Soufrière. One of the oldest, offering catamaran tours, is **Endless Summer Cruises** (tel: 758-450 8651, www.stlucia boattours.com).

Depending on the time of year St Lucia hosts numerous sailing events, many of them beginning or ending at Rodney Bay Marina (see http://stluciayachtclub.com/events). There are races round the island, to Martinique and back, or just off Reduit Beach while the Atlantic Rally for Cruisers is an annual race from the Canary Islands to St Lucia.

LAND SPORTS

CYCLING

There are mountain bike trips on the trails of **Treetop Adventure Park** (tel: 758-458 0908, www.adventuretoursst lucia.com) that run through the scenic countryside and dense beautiful forest, and stopping for a dip in the cooling Dennery waterfall. Not for the faint hearted are the bike trails that cut through the lush vegetation on the Anse Mamin Plantation. **Bike St Lucia** (tel: 758-457 1400, www.bikestlucia.com) has trails for all levels of experience. They vary in difficulty from yellow (lower intermediate), red (intermediate) to black (expert). The most challenging ride is Tinker's trail, which has a steep uphill and fast downhill track.

HIKING

Exploring the island interior on foot is one way to experience some of the breathtaking scenery that makes up the volcanic island's landscape. With almost year round warm sunshine and summer temperatures rising above 31°C (88°F), the high mountain and forest areas, where it is several degrees cooler, provide walkers with welcome relief from the heat.

Hiking along a tropical river

St Lucia has 77 sq km (30 sq miles) of protected forest land, which is the natural habitat of rare plants, trees, birds and wildlife. As a result walking tours are permitted only with an official guide. Forest walks and hikes vary in difficulty.

Joining a Bike St Lucia adventure

The **Edmund Forest Reserve** has a manned ranger station and a public toilet. A 3-hour hike along the reserve's strenuous walking trails leads deep into the forest, where you can enjoy the shade of tall ferns, blue mahoe, bamboo and mahogany laced with bromeliads, lianas and orchids. You can also see fabulous flora and fruit such as the bird of paradise, brightly coloured heliconia and hibiscus, banana and pineapple plants.

Visitors need to be fit to attempt the 4km (2.5-mile) **Enbas Saut Trail**, which takes walkers down 2,112 steps to two cascades that flow into clear pools below, and beyond to the Troumassée River and the hamlet of Micoud on the East Coast.

Nearby the lush canopied *Quilesse Forest Reserve* is the habitat of the rarely seen St Lucia parrot (*Amazona versicolor*), known locally as jacquot. The walking trails through this reserve can also provide glimpses of other indigenous island wildlife.

Travelling by ATV

The moderately taxing **Barre de L'Isle Trail** (1.6km/1 mile) cuts through the forest in an east to west direction and provides unforgettable panoramic views over the Cul-de-Sac and Mabouya valleys and out to the Atlantic Coast.

A short drive (30 minutes) southeast of Castries is the 5km (3-mile) **Piton Flore Nature Trail/Forestière Trail**. It follows an old French road through a mature forest with lush ferns and fig trees.

For more information about the island's forest reserves and other national heritage sites or to book a trail hike contact: **St Lucia Forestry Department** (tel: 758-468 5649, http://malff.com) or **St Lucia Heritage Tours** (tel: 758-458 1454, www.heritagetoursstlucia.org).

BIRDWATCHING

With such vast forested areas and a mountain landscape, visitors to St Lucia can spot some of the region's colourful and rare, indigenous and migratory birds. With patience and luck you may see some wonderful tropical birds such as the endangered St Lucia wren (*Troglodytes aedon mesoleucus*), St Lucia black finch (*Melanospiza richardsoni*), the white breasted thrasher (*Ramphocinclus brachyurus sanctaeluciae*) and the national bird, the St Lucia parrot (*Amazona versicolor*), with its bright blue face, green wings and a red patch across the throat and chest.

Several forest areas throughout the island are especially good for birdwatching, including the Millet Bird Sanctuary, Edmund Forest Reserve, Quilesse Forest Reserve, Grand Anse, Grand Bois Forest, Maria Islands Nature Reserve, Savannes Bay Nature Reserve and the Monkoté Mangrove swamp.

Birdwatching tours are best arranged through the Forestry Department (tel: 758-468 5649).

ATV TOURS
A tour through plantation land on an all-terrain vehicle (ATV) adds a touch of adventure to any trip. **ATV Paradise Tours Ltd** (Fond Estate, Micoud, tel: 758-455 3245, www.atvstlucia.

CRICKET

The official cricket season runs from January to July when there are inter-island, regional and international matches. There is an impressive national cricket ground in Beausejour, Gros Islet, the venue for some of the Cricket World Cup matches when the tournament was hosted by the West Indies in 2007. St Lucian female cricketers are valuable members of the women's West Indies team, but the men lagged behind until Darren Sammy was chosen for the West Indies tour of England in 2007. The Micoud-born cricketer was the first ever St Lucian selected for the men's senior team and he became captain of the West Indies in 2010.

com) take small groups with a maximum of four ATVs through Davie Estate where they grow tropical fruits, flowers and vegetables, with stops along the way for sampling and tasting and at the old sugar mill.

ZIP-LINING

There are several places offering zip-lining in addition to other attractions on site. **Rain Forest Adventures** (Chassin, tel: 758-458 5151; www.rainforestadventure.com) has some good lines through the forest in the northeast, while also offering a canopy tram tour, hiking and birdwatching. On the west coast, in full view of the Pitons, **Morne Coubaril Estate** (Soufrière, tel: 758-459 7340; www.stluciaziplining.com) has zip lines through the plantation and its fruit trees, as well as tours of the estate, hiking to a waterfall and horse riding. On the east coast, along

Rain Forest Adventures canopy tram tour

the Dennery River, is **Treetop Adventure Park** (Dennery, tel: 758-458 0908; www.adventure toursstlucia.com), with zip lines down the forested hillside, as well as bike tours, kayaking and a jeep safari.

GOLF

There is an 18-hole championship golf course at **St Lucia Golf Club** (Cap Estate, Rodney Bay, tel: 758-450 8523, www.stluciagolf.com) in the far north of the island. Clubs, balls and shoes can be hired, and 40-minute lessons are available on the driving range.

Christmas fireworks

A familiar sound at Christmas time in rural hill areas is the loud crack of bamboo bursting. Traditionally young men hollow out a piece of bamboo, insert a stick and plug the bamboo with a kerosene-soaked rag. When lit the noise of the bamboo bursting can be heard far away.

SHOPPING

There are two pricey shopping malls in Castries designed to attract cruise ship visitors: La Place Carenage and Pointe Seraphine, while in Rodney Bay there is Baywalk Mall with a variety of shops and a supermarket opposite the older JQ Mall, which also has a well-stocked supermarket. For souvenirs such as cocoa sticks, spices, hot sauces and other local specialities, try the market in Castries, at its busiest on a Saturday morning when farmers come to town. Crafts, T-shirts, hats, sarongs and beach wraps can be found in the Vendors' Arcade across the road (see page 31).

ART

St Lucia has no national gallery, but exhibitions of the work of local artists are mounted regularly. The **St Lucia National Archives Portrait Gallery** (Clark Avenue, Vigie; tel: 758-452 1654) has changing exhibitions of photographs and portraits of

A clothes shop in downtown Castries

eminent St Lucians from all walks of life, some painted by the most famous local artists, Cedric George and Dunstan St Omer.

Commercial galleries include: **Art and Antiques** (Pointe Seraphine, Castries, tel: 758-459 0891) which exhibits the work of Llewellyn Xavier and other local and international artists; **Artsibit Gallery** (corner of Brazil and Mongiraud streets, Castries, tel: 758-452 7865) has paintings, sculpture, prints and pottery from St Lucia and the Caribbean; **The Inner Gallery** (Reduit Beach Avenue, Rodney Bay Village, tel: 758-452 8728, www.facebook.com/theinnergallery) has a selection of work by artists from St Lucia and the Caribbean.

CRAFTS

The African influence is best seen through the crafts and art produced on the island, particularly the woodcarvings. Art in wood, of varying quality and size, can be found in artists' studios, markets and souvenir shops.

Sculptor and woodcarver Vincent Joseph Eudovic works at his Goodlands studio in the hills of Morne Fortune (see page 34). His beautiful abstract carvings are created from local woods such as laurier mabouey, teak, mahogany and red and white cedar. His son, Jallim Eudovic, is also carving himself an international reputation.

Choiseul is well-known for its distinctive clay pottery but also fine hand-woven baskets that are sturdy enough to take to market and aesthetically pleasing enough for an excursion to the beach. The craft centre at Choiseul (see page 71) sells the work of potters, basket-weavers and woodcarvers, who continue crafts handed down from generation to generation.

The ancient Indonesian art of batik is given a Caribbean flavour at Caribelle Batik. Fabric is printed with bright images taken straight from St Lucian wildlife and natural landscapes.

KWÉYÒL CULTURE AND FESTIVALS

The **Folk Research Centre** (Plas Wichès Folklò, Mount Pleasant; Mon–Fri 8.30am–4.30pm; tel: 758-452 2279; www.stluciafolk.org) stands near L'Anse Road off the Gros Islet Highway, north of the centre of Castries. The Centre houses a cultural archive and a small museum. The library has an excellent collection of history books, reference material, audio-visual recordings and priceless photographs. This is the island's best folk history and culture study centre, which was set up to promote and preserve traditional customs and the Kwéyòl language and art. It offers Kwéyòl language classes, school programmes, translation services, orthography, folk art production and exhibitions. There are numerous events and performances during La Rose, La Marguerite and Kwéyòl festivals and at Christmas, but it is especially busy in October during Creole heritage month, culminating in Jounen Kwéyòl at the end of the month.

CHILDREN'S ST LUCIA

There is no shortage of ways to entertain children of all ages and St Lucia is the ideal family holiday destination. The Caribbean beaches are perfect, with a range of sand colours to explore, and wonderfully warm water for playing in. Watersports providers cater for all ages and children will love learning to windsurf, sail or kayak. Snorkelling and learning about what is under the water is incredibly exciting and older children may want to learn to scuba dive. On land they can get an adrenaline rush on a zip line or a mountain biking excursion, work off some energy with a hike through the rainforest identifying birds and other creatures and learn about geology, mud and nasty smells at the Sulphur Springs. Whale watching and turtle watching trips are also great learning experiences.

Children always love the beach

The food on offer is great for kids, with plenty of carbohydrates (pizza, pasta, burgers) to keep up their energy levels as well as lots of tropical fruits, juices and ice creams to try. Health is not an issue as long as they are well hydrated and avoid sunburn. Take care between 11am–3pm, even on a cloudy day, and especially if out on a boat.

CALENDAR OF EVENTS

January Nobel Laureate Week (3rd week). Talks and lectures celebrating the two St Lucian Nobel Laureates, both born on 23 January: Sir Arthur Lewis and Derek Walcott.

22 February Independence Day celebrated with exhibitions, sporting events, concerts and talks.

May St Lucia Jazz Festival (variable). Held at mostly outdoor venues, concerts by local and international artists attract large crowds.

29 June St Peter's Day. Fishermen's Feast (Fete Peche) when all the fishing boats are decorated.

June, July Carnival (variable). St Lucia Carnival is a fun-filled celebration culminating with Mas Bands 'jumping-up' in colourful costumes and calypsonians vying for the crown of the Calypso Monarch. www.luciancarnival.com

30 August Feast of St Rose De Lima (La Rose, Fêt La Wòz). Dancing and singing by communities in traditional costumes.

October Thanksgiving Day (first Monday). Giving thanks for hurricane survival or the lack of a hurricane.

17 October Feast of La Marguerite. A church service followed by a parade with participants dressed as kings and queens, music, dancing, food and drink. Both La Rose and La Marguerite stem from secret societies set up by African slaves.

October Jounen Kwéyòl Entenasyonnal (International Creole Day) (last Sun). Activities are held throughout the month but culminate with celebrations in four or five communities with local food, crafts, music and cultural displays.

December Atlantic Rally for Cruisers. Cruising yachts start in Las Palmas, Gran Canaria, in November and race to Rodney Bay, arriving before Christmas for a season of parties and celebrations.

13 December National Day. St Lucy's Day, the patron saint of light is celebrated with the Festival of Lights and Renewal and a procession with lanterns.

25 December Christmas Day. A Christmas tradition is the equivalent of carol singers, who sing Creole songs to a chak chak band.

EATING OUT

In almost every aspect of St Lucian culture there is a colourful blend of African, Amerindian, French and British influences, and nowhere more so than in its cuisine, which is known as Creole. The tropical climate and fertile soil mean that the island enjoys a near endless bounty of nature from cassava, sweet potato and dasheen to fragrant nutmeg, cinnamon and ginger. The landscape is punctuated with rich farmland where bananas, pineapple, grapefruit, oranges and mangoes grow in abundance. There is also superb seafood from the surrounding Caribbean Sea and Atlantic Ocean. The market in Castries is a riot of colour and scents, well worth exploring to investigate the wealth of produce grown on the island or gathered from its surrounding waters. It is a feast for the eyes and nose as well as the taste buds; you can buy fruit and snacks for a picnic, sample a local lunch at a market stall or stock up on cocoa and spices to take home as edible souvenirs. A typical lunch will include meat of some sort, plantains, potatoes or other starchy vegetables, macaroni, rice and shredded lettuce, accompanied by fruit juice. This is the main meal of the day.

For those who do not care for island food at every meal, rest assured that most of St Lucia's restaurants in the tourist areas serve international or fusion cuisine. You can savour the very best beef steaks imported from the USA or Argentina, share a huge pizza with friends, grab a burger or go for a curry. The island can not support livestock farming to any great degree, so beef, lamb and dairy produce is usually imported, although you can find local pork, goat and chicken.

Breadfruit

The breadfruit was brought to the West Indies in 1793 by Captain Bligh (of *Mutiny on the Bounty* fame) and its large round fruit was useful to provide slaves with carbohydrates and vitamins A, B and C.

A wealth of spicy sauces for sale in Castries

Seafood has a distinct and intense flavour here, most likely because it is served so fresh. Fish such as snapper, mahi-mahi (also known as dorado or dolphin), wahoo, flying fish and tuna are all available, as are crab, spiny lobster (in season 1 September to 30 April) and conch (same season). The result is that mealtimes can often be a delicious cornucopia of fragrances and flavours. Weekly street parties at Anse la Raye, Dennery and Vieux Fort are fun places to try local, seasonal seafood. Fishermen bring the freshest catch of the day, including huge lobsters, to be cooked on barbecues made from oil drums, where you can pick whatever you fancy for dining under the stars.

Breakfast is usually available from 7am–10am, lunch noon–2pm and dinner 6pm – 10pm. Some restaurant kitchens stay open until 11pm, particularly if there is a bar attached, but generally late-night dining is not common. Castries is not known for its nightlife, although there are lots of places for

Catch of the day

lunch catering to the office workers and cruise ship visitors. The greatest concentration of restaurants is in the Rodney Bay area where most of the hotels are. These are of a good standard – some are excellent – and so varied that all tastes are accommodated. From beach bars to fine dining, there is a wide range for all budgets.

WHAT TO EAT

Many of the foods the Amerindian settlers grew and consumed are still around today, notably cassava, sweet potatoes, yam, corn, peppers, avocado, okra, peanuts, cashew nuts and pumpkin. The Amerindians delighted in roasted corn, and today it remains a popular and healthy snack. The island's street vendors roast the corn on barbecues, often until it is black.

Cassava bread is a St Lucian staple, first enjoyed by the Amerindians and later the enslaved West Africans, who brought with them their own version of the bread. Served as an accompaniment to a main meal or as a filling snack, modern cassava bread comes in a variety of flavours from sweet or cherry to smoked herring.

The island's national dish is green fig and saltfish, a tasty meal of seasoned salt cod and small green bananas, known locally as a fig. Also worth a try is hearty pumpkin soup or callaloo soup made from the green leaf of the dasheen, a common root vegetable. The leaves have a spinach-like appearance and can also be cooked up with onions and saltfish.

Saltfish was first introduced to the Caribbean as an easy-to-store, inexpensive source of protein for the slaves working the land and it was they who created imaginative ways to cook it. Making the best of what was on offer and what they could afford has inspired generations of Caribbean cooks, so it is little wonder that menus include dishes made from almost every imaginable part of a pig or cow.

Pigs' tails are a local speciality, cooked in a juicy stew. Other stews include pepperpot – a combination of meats, vegetables and hot peppers with cassava juice – while souse bouillon contains salt beef cooked with a spicy mix of onions,

MANGOES

Although there are more than 100 varieties of mango, just seven can be found in great numbers on St Lucia. Around 2,000 tons of the fruit are exported each year to as far afield as the UK. Of the seven common varieties only a few actually originate from St Lucia; they include the large juicy Cabishe, the Long and the Pa Louis mangoes. The sweet, orange-coloured Julie mango actually comes from Trinidad. Though closely associated with the region the mango, like the banana, is not indigenous. The fruit, be it sweet or tart, smooth or stringy in texture, can be juiced to produce a drink or made into ice cream or chutney.

beans, little dumplings and potatoes. Then there is cowheel soup and oxtail, chicken and beef, stewed, fried, baked or in mouthwatering curries.

The word 'provisions' on a menu indicates a variety of root or starchy vegetables, such as yams, sweet potatoes or tannia. Side dishes include breadfruit roasted or boiled, cut in slices or cubed in a salad, accras (spicy deep fried fishcakes made with salt cod), cassava, dasheen, sweet potato, yam, green fig, plantain, lentils, plain rice and rice and peas. These can be green or dried pigeon peas, black eye, split peas or lentils. Christophene, another local vegetable, is often served baked in a cheese sauce. Bakes are a fried dough patty filled with fish or corned beef, a popular snack bought in most bakeries.

Roti, a flat unleavened bread wrap that contains a spicy meat, fish or vegetarian filling, is a filling lunch. Originating in Trinidad where it was developed by immigrants from India,

SMALL BUT SWEET

Bananas grown in the Windward Islands are smaller and (some say) sweeter than the larger fruit from elsewhere. Although you can find them in supermarkets in the northern hemisphere, you will notice that they are sweeter here, because they have been allowed to ripen longer on the plant. Bananas picked for export are ripened artificially, which affects the flavour. Unripe, green bananas, known as green fig, are cooked, much like plantains, which are also eaten in St Lucia. The island is closely associated with the banana, a dominant crop for decades until the late 1990s, when farmers were forced to begin diversifying crops. Bananas are grown by small-scale farmers, either organically or with the minimum of chemicals. The plant takes 9–10 months to develop, and can propagate itself by producing suckers on its stem, which can be planted to produce another plant.

Local flavours

the roti has spread up the island chain and is more popular than the sandwich.

The island's food is flavoursome because of the seasonings used, of which onions, garlic, lime, peppers, thyme, ginger, clove, cinnamon and nutmeg are the most common. You will find a bottle of hot pepper sauce – made from scotch bonnet pepper – on almost every table, but be careful when adding it to your food as the strength of the sauce can vary greatly from mild to fiery.

FRUITS

Well-known for its small sweet bananas, the island also produces tropical fruits including guava, soursop (chirimoya, guanabana), mango (see box), papaya (paw paw), pineapple, orange, grapefruit, lime, passionfruit, tamarind, sapodilla (zapote), carambola (star fruit), sugar apple (custard apple, sweetsop) and coconut. Fruit is everywhere, made in to juice,

Breakfast with a view

ice cream, a pickle or chutney. Hotels usually offer a wide range of fruits at their breakfast buffets, including melons.

SWEETS AND PASTRIES

The region's love affair with sugar stems back to the 17th-century plantation era when St Lucia began its sugar industry. Those with a sweet tooth won't be disappointed with a choice of sweets and pastries as different as tangy tamarind balls and coconut sugar cakes, cinnamon turnovers and banana bread. And don't forget the island fruit preserves such as guava jelly. Cocoa and chocolate are now firmly on the tourist trail, with several old cacao plantations around Soufrière having been renovated and opened for visitors with demonstrations of the bean to bar process. Not only can you eat and drink it, but you can be massaged with cocoa butter or defoliated with cocoa nibs. The possibilities are endless. So important has cocoa become, that August has been dedicated Cocoa Heritage Month.

WHAT TO DRINK

Refreshing fruit juices abound, including orange, mango, pineapple, grapefruit, lime, guava and passionfruit. Unripe, green coconuts are full of refreshing, sterile water, sold by roadside vendors, who will hack off the top with a machete and provide you with a drinking straw. The water and jelly round the edge of the shell is full of potassium, magnesium and antioxidants. Tamarind is a bitter sweet drink made from the pulp around the seeds inside the pods (legumes) of the tamarind tree and contains calcium as well as B vitamins. At Christmas it is traditional to make the bright red sorrel drink, naturally coloured by the petals of the sorrel flower and spiced with cinnamon, cloves, ginger and orange peel. St Lucians also drink a variety of herbal teas, often for medicinal reasons, and a knowledge of herbs and their uses is passed down through the generations. Cocoa tea is drunk at breakfast, but do not expect it to be like the commercial varieties of hot chocolate. Cocoa beans are dried, fermented and roasted before being ground and compacted into cocoa sticks or balls, often with spices such as cinnamon and nutmeg. These are then grated and added to hot water (or milk), sweetened to taste and served as cocoa tea.

Islanders are rightly proud of their rum. St Lucia Distillers produces a selection of dark and white rums at its factory in the Roseau Valley (see page 51). The dark rums include Bounty, most commonly used in cocktails and punches, TOZ Gold and Elements 8 Gold.

Know your measures

In a rum shop, a 'flask' is a small, flat bottle holding enough for four people to share, maybe with a mixer; a 'nip' serves three, a 'half nip' serves two, while a 'shot' is an individual measure. A 'mix' is rum and falernum, a spiced syrup (alcoholic or non-alcoholic) from Barbados.

Connoisseurs can try the extra-aged Admiral Rodney and Chairman's Reserve. Crystal is a white rum, used in cocktails, while Denros is a double strength 160° proof rum (good for rubbing on aching joints even if you can't drink it).

In the island rum shops (known as *cabawe*) rum is drunk straight up or on the rocks, but the uninitiated can enjoy theirs in a blend of tropical fruit juices or with other mixers. There are also ready-made rum punches such as Smugglers rum punch, spiced rum such as Kwèyòl Spiced Rum and rum-based liqueurs such as Crème la Caye, Nutz & Rum (a peanut blend) and Orange Bliss. There are some 20 blended, flavoured or unadulterated rum products in all. Less potent is the local beer: Piton. Brewed in Vieux Fort, it is a lager, best drunk very cold. A shandy is usually a mixture of beer and ginger ale, but a Piton shandy can be with lemon, sorrel or ginger.

Admire Petit Piton while supping a mojito

PLACES TO EAT

You will never be far from somewhere to eat, but the greatest concentration of restaurants is in Rodney Bay, where a week's holiday is not long enough to try them all. Below is a selection of restaurants, divided into three categories according to the price of a main course:

$$$ = over US$30   **$$** = US$15–30   **$** = less than US$15

CASTRIES

Auberge Seraphine $$–$$$ *Vielle Bay, Pointe Seraphine; tel: 758-453 2073; www.aubergeseraphine.com.* A lovely place with an international menu, popular with business visitors and tourists. Overlooks the marina, best at twilight when you can watch the yachts, roosting egrets, and departing cruise ships. Open daily for breakfast, lunch and dinner.

Brown Sugar $$ *Vigie Cove, tel: 758-458 1031;* www.brownsugar restaurantandbar.com. Off the beaten track but delightful outdoor waterfront dining overlooking the boats in the harbour. Casual and friendly, run by a husband and wife team. Good food with an island emphasis and excellent service. Open daily 11am–2.30pm, 7–11pm for food, bar open all day.

The Coal Pot $$$ *Vigie Marina; tel: 758-452 5566;* www.coalpot restaurant.com. French cuisine with a Caribbean twist. One of the oldest restaurants, popular with local business people for lunch and visitors for dinner. Open Mon–Fri for lunch and dinner, Sat dinner only.

The Pink Plantation House $$ *The Morne, Chef Harry Drive; tel: 758-452 5422.* Up on the hill in lush gardens overlooking Castries harbour with a pleasant breeze and glorious view from the veranda where tables are set. The food is varied, tasty and plentiful while the service is attentive and friendly. Owned by a ceramicist; you can see her workshop and buy her work. Open Mon–Thu 11.30am–3pm, Fri 11.30am–9pm, Sun 9am–noon. Reservations advised.

RODNEY BAY AND NORTH

Big Chef $$$ *Reduit Drive, Rodney Bay, tel: 758-450 0210; www.big chefsteakhouse.com.* Popular, busy and with a great atmosphere, here you can eat the most tender, aged, Angus beef steaks plus a variety of seafood and fish, accompanied by a good selection of international wines. Open daily from 6pm. An attached tapas bar, Tapas on the Bay, www.tapasonthebay.com, has a selection of appetizers, sherries and cigars with a happy hour 4–6pm.

Blue Monkey Café $ *JQ Mall, Rodney Bay, tel: 758-4854600.* There are good coffee and juices on offer here – the cappuccinos are popular. Also good for breakfast, lunch or a later meal. Filling breakfasts include stuffed toasted baguettes or burger buns which will set you up for the day. For lunch try a hearty soup, a roti or a tasty salad. Outdoor seating only but umbrellas for shade. Open daily 7am–10pm.

The Cliff at Cap $$$ *Cap Maison, Smugglers Cove Drive, Cap Estate, tel: 758-457 8681; www.thecliffatcap.com.* Fine dining with nouveau French Caribbean fusion cuisine in a pleasant clifftop setting overlooking the sea. Smart, but families welcome and children eat for free if eating with their parents, or there is an early sitting for youngsters 5.30–6.30pm on request. Open for breakfast, lunch and dinner.

Delirius $$–$$$ *Rodney Bay Village, tel: 758-451 3354; www.deliriusstlucia.com.* Primarily a bar with award-winning bartenders, colourful with great cocktails and other drinks, but also offering a range of food, from burgers, ribs and steaks to their signature fresh fish and seafood. Conveniently located in the middle of the nightlife strip, it has a lively vibe. Open for lunch and dinner.

Elegance Café $$–$$$ *Massade, Gros Islet, tel: 758-450 9864; www.facebook.com/Elegancecafesaintlucia.* Unpretentious but comfortably smart restaurant with indoor or outdoor dining and bar. The Indian chef creates a range of delicious and flavoursome dishes, while more international options are also available. Special requests happily accommodated. Open Mon–Sat lunch and dinner until 9pm.

Flavours of the Grill $$ *Marie Therese St, Gros Islet, tel: 758-284 7906; www.grillflavours.com.* A casual spot set in a traditional painted wooden cottage with some tables on the veranda outside and some indoors, but all open to the air. Hearty menu items include grilled fish, chicken, curry goat and sometimes lobster, served with local side dishes such as ground provisions or rice and peas. Reservations advised. Open Mon–Thu, Sat noon–10pm, Fri noon–1am.

Jambe de Bois $–$$ *Pigeon Island National Landmark, tel: 758-452 0321.* Seafront cafe serving St Lucian specialities in the park. A pleasant place to take a break after hiking up the hill, to sit and watch the boating activity in the bay, whether for drinks, lunch or later for dinner with reservation. There is good snorkelling just offshore, so you can make a day of it. Not a place to go if you are in a hurry.

Jacques Waterfront Dining (Froggie Jacques) $$$ *Rodney Bay Village, tel: 758-458 1900; www.jacquesrestaurant.com.* Lovely setting at the end of Reduit Beach by the entrance to the marina, waterfront dining. A long-established restaurant offering fusion French and Caribbean food, although it has relocated since the original Vigie building burned down. Open daily noon–3pm, 6–10pm.

The Naked Fisherman $$–$$$ *Cap Maison Resort & Spa, Smugglers Cove, Cap Estate, tell 758-457 8694; http://nakedfishermanstlucia.com.* A pricey beach bar and grill set on a delightful cove. There are 92 steps down to the beach and people tend to stay a while once arrived, before climbing back up again. The food is good and varied, from gourmet burgers and salads to elegant seafood dishes for lunch with extra meat dishes for supper. Open daily, lunch 12.30pm–4pm, dinner Thu–Sat 6–9.30pm.

Razmataz $–$$$ *Rodney Bay, opposite the Royal St Lucian Hotel, tel: 758-452 9800; www.razmatazrestaurant.com.* Long-established tandoori restaurant with a chef from Nepal, popular with British tourists needing a good curry. Lots of flavoursome dishes and good-sized portions. Open air dining with Indian décor and tables on covered veranda. Happy hour 5–7pm with light bites at the bar. Open 5–11pm, closed Tue.

Spice of India $$–$$$ *Bay Walk Mall, Rodney Bay Village, tel: 758-458 4243;* http://spiceofindiastlucia.com. Excellent Indian food prepared by chefs from India with imported ingredients, while taking advantage of local delicacies such as crab and shrimp. Good meat dishes but also good for vegetarians with lots of tasty options. Friendly and hospitable service, very popular so reservations advised. Open daily except Mon lunch, noon–3.45pm, 6pm–onwards.

La Terrasse $$–$$$ *Seagrape Ave, Rodney Bay, tel: 758-572 0389;* www.laterrassestlucia.com. A small and intimate inn with romantic French restaurant. French chef Thomas prepares delicious and authentic dishes. Reservations recommended. Open from 6.30pm, closed Tue.

The Wharf $–$$ *Gros Islet Highway, Choc Bay, tel: 758-450 4844.* A casual beach bar and restaurant next to Villa Beach Cottages, serving snacks such as sandwiches or roti, or full meals with local specialities as well as more international fare. Relaxed and friendly, it can get lively at night when there is often karaoke or live music and dancing. Beach chairs available if you want to spend the day there. Open daily 9am–late.

Wingz-N-Tingz $–$$ *Seagrape Ave, Rodney Bay, tel: 758-451 8200;* wingzntingz@hotmail.com. A good place to come for fast food: marinated chicken wings cooked on the barbeque with a variety of sauces, although there are other dishes such as catch of the day and the green banana salad should be tried. Excellent fresh juices or a cold Piton beer to wash it down. Occasional live music.

MARIGOT BAY

Rainforest Hideaway $$$ *Marigot Bay, north side, tel: 758-451 4485;* www.rainforesthideawaystlucia.com. Reached by complimentary ferry boat, this is a romantic location on the water. Food is good, using local ingredients, and the service is exemplary. Come for a special night out, perhaps by water taxi from the north – a private sunset cruise. Live entertainment two nights a week.

Reservations required, open daily Dec–mid-May from 6pm, less often in low season.

SOUFRIÈRE AND ENVIRONS

The Beacon $-$$ *Columbette, Soufrière, tel: 758-286 9659*; www.facebook.com/pages/The-Beacon-Restaurant-Tranquil-Villas-Maranatha-Garden. On the main road from the north to Soufrière and a convenient place to stop for lunch while on a tour of the island, so often busy with coach parties. Perched up high, it has a fantastic view over the town and bay to the Pitons beyond. Lunch is usually a set-price buffet of local food, all tasty and well prepared. Their peaceful Maranatha Garden has a beautiful display of tropical plants.

Boucan Restaurant & Bar $$-$$$ *Hotel Chocolat, Rabot Estate, tel: 758-457 1624*, www.hotelchocolat.com. This restaurant definitely has the 'wow' factor. It is on a working cocoa plantation where the menu is cocoa-inspired for both sweet and savoury dishes and drinks, using locally-sourced, seasonal ingredients. Perched high up with spectacular views of the Pitons, the minimalist design allows you to concentrate on the gourmet food or your sunset cocktail. Open daily for breakfast, lunch, dinner or just drinks.

Le Café $-$$ *26 Bay St, Soufrière, tel: 758-723 0750.* A small, friendly café offering breakfast, lunch and snacks with lovely home made cakes and good coffee and drinks. At night, by reservation, you can have a candlelit, set price, three-course meal including wine. Order in advance which meat you want and it comes with all the local accompaniments, such as provisions, lentils, macaroni and vegetables.

Dasheene $$$ *Ladera Resort, tel: 758-459 6600*; www.ladera.com. Award-winning restaurant with innovative dishes using fresh local ingredients. Breathtaking views of the Pitons. Live music at dinner. Open for breakfast, lunch, tea, dinner, Sun brunch buffet.

Fedo's $ *New Development, Soufrière, tel: 758-459 5220.* In the residential area, off the road which leads to the Botanical

Gardens, ask locally for directions. Look for a blue and white painted house. Local lunches, everything fresh, tasty, filling and cheap. A good place to try island home cooking. Open for lunch Mon–Sat.

Hummingbird $$–$$$ *Hummingbird Beach Resort, Soufrière, tel: 758-459 7985;* http://istlucia.co.uk. A pleasant spot by the sea with a view of the Pitons across Soufrière Bay. Good for a meal or just drinks to watch the sunset from the Lifeline Bar. Creole specialities and the fish and seafood are fresh and tasty. Service can be slow. Open for lunch and dinner.

Jade Mountain $$$ *Jade Mountain, Soufrière, tel: 758-459 4000;* www.jademountainstlucia.com. Luxury hotel restaurant, reservations required. Lunch is the better option because you can enjoy the spectacular view of the Pitons from the restaurant perched on top of this futuristic resort. Stay until sunset and leave when it gets dark. Dinner is a set menu and expensive.

Jardin Cacao Restaurant at Fond Doux Holiday Plantation $$–$$$ *Soufrière, tel: 758-459 7545;* www.fonddouxestate.com. Lush tropical setting in plantation gardens with birds and wildlife. Organic fruits and vegetables from the estate are used in the cooking. Many visitors are on a plantation tour with a buffet lunch included, but you can also have à la carte – the restaurant is open for breakfast, lunch and dinner for hotel guests and others with reservations. Live music Sat evening.

The Mango Tree $$–$$$ *Stonefield Estate Resort, Soufrière, tel: 758-459 7037;* www.stonefieldresort.com. On the hillside with views of Petit Piton. Relaxed atmosphere with local dishes such as spicy roti, using homegrown organic produce. Vegan options. Barbecue and entertainment on Thu, steel pan on Sat. Open daily 7.30am–10pm.

Martha's Tables $$ *Jalousie Rd, Soufrière, tel: 758-459 7270;* www. marthastables.com. Under Petit Piton, this is a good place to stop for a local lunch if you're in the area. This is home cooking – choose your main dish and lots of side dishes come with it. Open Mon-Fri 11.30am-3pm.

Orlando's $$$ *Cemetery Rd, Fond Bernier, Soufrière, tel: 758-459 5955;* www.orlandosrestaurantstl.com. Small, cosy and intimate, this is the best independent restaurant in the area. Orlando serves up delectable gourmet creole meals, tasting menus and simpler fare for lunch, using ingredients bought in Soufrière market. Excellent service. Open Tue–Sun from 6pm, also lunch from noon with reservation.

VIEUX FORT AND SOUTH COAST

The Reef Beach Café $–$$ *Anse De Sables, tel: 758-454 3418;* www.slucia.com/reef. Casual beach cafe with Caribbean fare such as saltfish, bakes, seafood salad and T-bone steak; there is also an à la carte menu available for dinner. Internet access and wheelchair access.

EAST COAST

Whispering Palm $$–$$$ *Fox Grove Inn, Mon Repos, tel: 758-455 3271;* www.foxgroveinn.com. A good lunch stop if touring this side of the island. Eat indoors or on the balcony for lovely views down to the east coast. Open daily for breakfast, lunch and dinner.

A–Z TRAVEL TIPS

A Summary of Practical Information

A

ACCOMMODATION

St Lucia has a reputation for expensive all-inclusive accommodation, but in fact there is a choice of places to stay, with something for every budget, from large all-inclusive resorts or luxury, boutique hotels to small, intimate inns and basic bed and breakfasts. Selfcatering apartments and luxury villas are also available to rent. Most of the resorts are in the north, the drier end of the island, which is where you also find the best restaurants and bars for convenient nightlife around Rodney Bay. Around Soufriere there are some very classy places to stay, where designers have made the most of the dramatic landscape to provide stunning views of the Pitons from the luxurious rooms.

Basic bed and breakfasts run by St Lucians who open up their homes to visitors are popular with budget-conscious travellers who don't mind staying off the beaten track and don't need the creature comforts offered by the upmarket resorts. Local people will also be able to point you in the direction of little-known sights and the best places to enjoy authentic Creole cuisine. If you are staying in a rural area or far from reliable public transport links you are best advised to rent a sturdy vehicle, or employ a guide, because taxi fares can mount up.

AIRPORTS

Long distance scheduled and charter flights, such as trans-Atlantic flights, fly in to **Hewanorra International Airport** (UVF) at Vieux Fort in the south, 67km (42 miles) from Castries. If you are staying at a hotel in the far north of the island be prepared for a scenic journey of up to 2 hours to get to your destination. Another, smaller airport, the **George F.L. Charles Airport** (SLU) is located at Vigie, on the outskirts of Castries, which receives inter-island flights. Airlines using the Vigie airport include LIAT, Air Caraïbes, Winair and

American Eagle. Daily arrivals and departure information can be found on www.slaspa.com. There is a helicopter shuttle from Hewanorra to George F.L. Charles Airport (**St Lucia Helicopters Ltd**, tel: 453 6950; www.stluciahelicopters.com). It is not a cheap option but it does cut travelling time right down to 10 minutes for the trip between the two airports.

B

BICYCLE RENTAL

St Lucia is not easy for cyclists. The roads are steep, twisty, potholed and traffic moves fast, often on the wrong side of the road. Watch out for storm drains. Bikes and scooters can be rented from **Pirate Rentals**, Rodney Bay, tel: 758-724 5111, www.pirate-rentals.com. Off-road cycling for tourists is offered by **Bike St Lucia**, tel: 758-457 1400, www.bikestlucia.com, on trails at Anse Mamin Plantation, near Soufrière, and by **Palm Services Rainforest Cycling Adventure**, tel: 758-458 0908, www.adventuretoursstlucia.com, at Errard Plantation on the east coast.

BUDGETING FOR YOUR TRIP

Getting to St Lucia. The cheapest direct scheduled return fares from London in high season are around £600 with either British Airways or Virgin Atlantic, although good value deals including accommodation as well as flights are available if you prefer a package holiday.

Accommodation. High season is 15 December–15 April, when prices are at their highest. Substantial discounts can be found at other times of the year, particularly during hurricane season. The cheapest accommodation is in self-catering apartments, which will cost US$30–50 a night depending on location and time of year. The most expensive rooms come with a spectacular view of the Pitons and cost over US$1,000 a night. There are plenty of options in between, but all come with tax of 20 percent.

Meals. If you are self-catering, a visit to the market will reveal a wealth of seasonal tropical fruits and vegetables at a fraction of the price you would pay at home. You can also eat economically at stalls in the Castries market to sample local dishes or at bars and family restaurants around the island. Prices in international-style restaurants in tourist areas or in hotels are much higher at around US$30–40 for a main course. Rum and rum-based cocktails are relatively cheap, but wine or imported spirits are expensive.

Local transport. Bus transport is cheap and easy to use. Short journeys cost as little as EC$1.50 (US$0.55), rising to a maximum of EC$8 (US$3) from one end of the island to the other. However, they do not always go where you want nor when, so taxi or car hire may be a better option, depending on what you want to do. A taxi from Castries to Gros Islet costs US$25 and from Hewanorra Airport to Rodney Bay US$75. A day's tour of the island is about US$200–250, depending on how far you go and for how long. Fares are set by the Government but you should always verify it in advance and check in which currency it is quoted.

Incidentals. Excursions are likely to be your biggest expense. A 2-hour sunset cruise costs US$60 per person including drinks, while a day sail including lunch, land tours and snorkelling is US$110. Whale watching boat tours are US$50–60 for three hours. An activity such as scuba diving is US$70–90 for two tanks, depending on how much gear you need to hire and whether transfers are included. Popular land-based activities such as segway tours around Rodney Bay start from US$85, while zip-lining ranges from US$40–85, depending on which option you choose.

C

CAR HIRE

In St Lucia you drive on the left. Visiting drivers must be over 25 years old and under 65 and should possess an international driver's licence (with an official stamp from the Immigration Department) or obtain a temporary driving permit, which is valid for three months, by presenting a current driving licence at the main police station (Bridge Street, Castries). The car rental company can also process a temporary permit, for which there is a charge of US$21 (EC$54). The wearing of seat belts is compulsory.

There is a choice of car rental companies with offices at the airports and in many resorts. Most will deliver the vehicle to your hotel and collect it at the end of the rental period. Daily rental rates are around US$50 for a car and US$75 for a SUV, but there is a 15% tax added to everything. It can be cheaper to rent in advance and in high season this is more reliable. The major international agents are: **Avis**, tel: 758-452 2700, www.avisstlucia.com; **Budget**, tel: 758-452 9887, http://budgetstlucia.com; **Hertz**, tel: 758-452 0679; www.hertzcaribbean.com.

CLIMATE

St Lucia has a tropical, humid climate with warm sunshine most of the year, cooled by northeastern trade winds. During the tourist high season (December to April) temperatures can reach 28–31°C (82–88°F) accompanied by a light breeze and short showers. The hottest months are June to August, while December and January are the coolest, when night and early morning temperatures can drop to 21°C (69°F). It is several degrees cooler in the rainforest and mountain villages, and colder still on the mountain peaks.

Rainy season. The rainy season runs from June to the end of November and is characterised by sporadic heavy showers. The annual rainfall can be up to three times higher in the mountains in the south (3,450mm/136 inches) than on the coast in the north (1,500mm/59 inches).

Tropical weather hazards. Storms are the most damaging weather phenomenon, but St Lucia's marinas and sheltered harbours on the Leeward (Caribbean) coast are popular with the sailing fraternity. However, the hilly terrain means St Lucia is particularly susceptible to mudslides caused by torrential rain, which often lead to casualties and huge farming losses.

Hurricanes. The hurricane season is generally between June and November, coinciding with the rainy season. Despite St Lucia falling technically into the Caribbean's hurricane belt, most hurricanes pass to the northwest of the island and the rare ones which make landfall are usually category 1 or 2 strength. For more information, see below:

Category 1: 74–95mph (119–153kph).
Category 2: 96–110mph (154–177kph).
Category 3: 111–130mph (178–209kph).
Category 4: 131–155mph (210–249kph).
Category 5: over 155mph (249kph).

In the event of a hurricane, stay indoors once it begins buffeting your area. When the eye (the low-pressure area at the center of a hurricane) passes over, there will be a temporary lull in wind and rain for up to half an hour or more. This is not the end of the storm, which will in fact resume (possibly with even greater force) from the opposite direction. Wait for the all-clear from the authorities before starting to venture out of your shelter.

	J	F	M	A	M	J	J	A	S	O	N	D
°C	26	25	26	27	28	28	28	28	28	28	27	26
°F	79	77	79	81	82	82	82	82	82	82	81	79

CLOTHING

Stick to cool and comfortable attire in the heat. Wearing skimpy shorts, skirts or beachwear while sightseeing and shopping in town is considered inappropriate and should be avoided. Most restaurants prefer their guests to dress elegantly casual, however some of the more upmarket establishments may require men to wear a jacket and occasionally a tie.

In winter the evenings can be cool, as can the air-conditioning, so it's best to carry a light cardigan or wrap; don't forget to take a lightweight umbrella or raincoat to protect you from brief showers during the rainy season.

CRIME AND SAFETY

St Lucia is a relatively safe island but crime, especially petty theft, certainly exists. By all means relax while on holiday but don't leave home without your common sense. Keep an eye on personal possessions and important documents when wandering in the markets and the busy resort areas; keep your money in a safe place, and leave your expensive jewellery at home or in the hotel safe. If you are renting a car keep valuables out of sight, preferably locked in the boot, and don't offer lifts to strangers. Avoid the beaches and out-of-the-way sidestreets after dark.

It is likely that you will be approached by vendors offering anything from hair braiding to crafts and a variety of souvenirs on the beach and at tourist attractions. If you are interested in what's on offer then haggle for an agreeable price, but if not don't waste people's time. A firm but polite "no thank you" is usually sufficient to deter any further advances.

D

DISABLED TRAVELLERS

Facilities for disabled visitors are few and far between, although some of the newer and larger hotels and resorts will be better equipped. In Castries and elsewhere the curbs and pavements can be high and difficult for wheelchair users and the physically challenged to negotiate, but nevertheless, there are many accessible visitor attractions on the island. Check in advance that your hotel has the facilities you require and that the places you want to visit can accommodate your needs.

DRIVING

Hiring a car gives you the greatest flexibility when driving around St Lucia, but it is more relaxing to hire a driver/guide for an island tour. You can negotiate an itinerary, you don't have to worry about twisty mountain roads or losing your way and you will receive a wealth of information about the island.

Car hire companies can often assist with arranging a driver, or ask at your hotel.

Road conditions. The government has invested heavily in road improvements in recent years and generally major roads and bridges are in good condition. However, rural roads can be potholed and may require four-wheel drive.

In the rainy season there are often landslides which can block or damage roads, so if there has been a storm you should seek local advice, particularly before driving down the west coast of St Lucia. Avoid driving after dark where possible; street lighting can be poor and oncoming vehicles often do not dip their headlights, making conditions more hazardous.

Rules and regulations. Driving is on the left, as in the UK, although the steering wheel may be on either side. At roundabouts give way to traffic already on the circle coming from your right. Seat belts are compulsory for all passengers. The speed limit is 30mph on highways, 15mph in towns, although this is widely disregarded.

Fuel costs. Filling stations are open from around 6.30–7am and stay open until about 8pm, Mon–Sat. A few open on Sun in the afternoon. Prices are set by the government in line with international prices. Unleaded fuel is about US$1.30 a litre, US$5.90 per gallon. Diesel is a bit cheaper.

E

ELECTRICITY

220 volts, 50 cycles AC and 110 volts, 60 cycles AC.

EMBASSIES AND CONSULATES

British High Commission, 2nd floor Francis Compton Building, Waterfront, Castries, tel: 758-452 2484; email: britishhc@candw.lc
US Embassy, located in Barbados, at US Embassy Rd, Bridgetown, tel: (246) 227 4000, http://barbados.usembassy.gov.

EMERGENCIES

The emergency number for Police, Fire and Ambulance is **911**.

ETIQUETTE

As in the Caribbean in general, good manners go a long way in St Lucia. 'Please;, 'thank you', and a respectful and friendly demeanor are expected from everyone. 'Hello', 'goodbye', 'good morning' and 'good night' are used in every situation, be it your hotel, a local bar, a restaurant or when passing strangers on the road. If you need to ask for directions, always greet the person you're asking first. Be sure to ask for permission before taking pictures of people.

G

GAY AND LESBIAN TRAVELLERS

Homosexual acts are legal for women but illegal for men, with penalties of up to 10 years in prison. St Lucian society is deeply conservative and religious and there have been violent homophobic attacks on gay St Lucians. There is no overtly gay scene, although many bars, restaurants and some resorts are gay friendly where tourists are concerned. You are advised to be discreet with your partner with no overt displays of affection in public places.

GETTING THERE

Air travel. The frequency of flights varies according to the season and many charter flights stop in the summer months and in the hurricane season. Schedules usually change mid-April. There are frequent flights from London Gatwick with both Virgin Atlantic and British Airways, while Thomas Cook Airlines fly weekly from Manchester. From the US there are direct flights from JFK New York and Boston with Jet Blue, from Miami with American Airlines, from Charlotte and Philadelphia with US Airways and from Atlanta and New York with Delta. Air Canada, Air Transat, Sunwing and WestJet fly from Toronto, Canada. Air Canada flies from Montréal. There are lots of flights connecting St Lucia with other islands in the Caribbean if you want to island hop with a regional airline, such as Air Caraïbes, LIAT, Caribbean Airlines or American Eagle.

By sea. L'Express des Iles has a high-speed catamaran car ferry service linking St Lucia with Dominica and the French islands of Martinique, Guadeloupe, Les Saintes and Marie Galante, usually crossing three times a week. Travelling time is short enough to justify hopping over to a neighbouring island for a day or even a weekend, but remember that this is an international crossing and you should take your passport. Avoid island hopping on the day you are leaving St Lucia because there is no guarantee that your ferry will return in time for you to make an airline connection. The agent in St Lucia, **Cox & Company Ltd**, has an office at the ferry terminal on La Toc Road in Castries (Mon–Fri 8am–6pm, tel: 456 5022/23/24, www.express-des-iles.com). St Lucia is a popular port of call for cruise ships starting from Florida, San Juan, Puerto Rico and Barbados. The port of entry is Castries and the view across the bay as the ship approaches is stunning. Cruise ships dock at Pointe Seraphine or Place Carenage, either side of Castries harbour, and there is duty-free shopping at both locations.

GUIDES AND TOURS

There are lots of tours available on land and by sea, half or whole day, for which your hotel or the Tourist Board will have details, or you can negotiate a tour with a taxi driver, most of whom make excellent guides.

Heritage Tours (tel: 758-458 1454, www.heritagetoursstlucia.org) is a co-operative of tourist sites with a strong community and heritage element offering a range of tours from Créole food and drink specialities to hiking, birdwatching or turtle watching, as well as more historical and cultural tours.

St Lucia Reps & Sunlink Tours (tel: 758-452 8232, www.stlucia reps.com) offer a full range of tours and excursions for cruise ship passengers and people staying on the island.

The **St Lucia National Trust** (tel: 758-452 5005, www.slunatrust. org) and its affiliate, **Eco-South Tours** (tel: 758-454 5014, ecosouth toursinc@gmail.com), offer nature tours of the Maria Islands and other natural attractions in the southeast.

H

HEALTH AND MEDICAL CARE

The main public medical facility on the island for residents and visitors was the large Victoria Hospital in Castries (tel: 758-452 2421), but this is now being replaced by the construction of the 116-bed New National Hospital (NNH), with a wide range of facilities and departments. Construction is complete and transitioning and equipping works were undertaken in 2014. When NNH is complete, the A&E Department of Victoria Hospital and the Castries Health Centre will be merged and called the Castries Urban Polyclinic.

Private hospitals on the island include St Jude's Hospital in Vieux Fort (tel: 758-454 6041) and the small Tapion Hospital in the south of Castries (tel: 758-459 2000), both of which have emergency services available to visitors. Elsewhere there are medical centres and clinics in Soufrière (tel: 758-459 7258/5001) and Dennery (tel: 758-453 3310).

L

LANGUAGE

Although St Lucia has been a British territory since 1814 and the official language is English, FrenchCreole (Kwéyòl) is spoken by more than 90 percent of people in informal arenas and, due to a drive to preserve and promote Creole traditions, is increasingly used in official circles as well. See page 12.

M

MAPS

There are several maps of the island distributed free in hotels and restaurants as well as in the tourist information booths and car hire companies. These are generally adequate for getting around the island on main roads and have local attractions clearly marked. Skyviews, www.skyviews.com, is one of the best, funded by advertising. For a more detailed topographical map, there is the Ordnance Survey map of St Lucia, dating from 1991, while the best road map is the Gizi Map, 2008.

MEDIA

St Lucia's newspapers can be read in print or online: *The Star*, http://stluciastar.com; *The Voice*, www.thevoiceslu.com; *The St Lucia Mirror*, www.stluciamirroronline.org. Online-only newspapers include *St Lucia Times*, www.stluciatimes.com and *St Lucia News Online*, www.stlucianewsonline.com. *Tropical Traveller*, a monthly magazine, promotes restaurants and gives information about upcoming events, and a biannual magazine, *Visions of St Lucia*, has listings and features about the island's attractions. Both are distributed through hotels.

There are nine local television channels, including Choice39 TV and DBS. St Lucia also receives a host of programmes from the US via satellite.

The island has 13 radio stations including Radio St Lucia, Radio 100 Helen FM, Radio Caribbean International and Hot FM, which broadcast local news and music.

MONEY

Currency. The official currency of St Lucia is the Eastern Caribbean dollar (EC$), which is pegged to the US dollar. The US dollar and all major credit cards and travellers' cheques are accepted in most places including restaurants and shops, especially in the resort areas. EC dollars are produced in denominations of $100, $50, $20, $10 and $5 notes and $1, 25¢, 10¢, 5¢, 2¢ and 1¢ coins.

Currency exchange. There are foreign exchange and banking facilities in Castries, Rodney Bay, Vieux Fort, Soufrière and at Hewanorra International Airport, which is usually open from 12.30pm until the last flight leaves.

Credit cards. Large hotels, shops and restaurants accept credit cards, but bars and small businesses operate in cash. Banks have ATMs and accept all major international credit and debit cards.

O

OPENING TIMES

Banks are generally open Monday to Thursday 8am–2pm, and until 5pm on Friday, while in Rodney Bay they are open on Saturday until noon. Government offices open 8.30am–4pm, but close for lunch 12.30–1.30pm. Shops open Mon–Fri 8am–5pm and on Saturday until 12.30pm. Supermarkets operate extended opening hours.

P

POLICE

The main police station is located on Bridge Street, Castries (tel: 758-452 2854). In Rodney Bay the police station is beside the St Lucia Yacht Club on Reduit Beach.

POST OFFICES

The main post office in the capital, Castries, is located on Bridge Street; there you can buy stamps and phonecards. Rodney Bay Mall and Gablewoods Mall have post office counters. There are also small post offices in most towns and generally they are open Monday to Friday 8.30am–4.30pm.

PUBLIC HOLIDAYS

1 January New Year's Day
2 January New Year's Holiday
22 February Independence Day
March/April (variable) Easter
1 May Labour Day; Whitsun (variable); Corpus Christi (variable)
1 August Emancipation Day
1 October Thanksgiving
13 December National Day
25 December Christmas Day
26 December Boxing Day

T

TELEPHONES

The international country code for St Lucia is **758**. Coin and card public phone boxes are found around the island. Mobile phones can be rented from specialist suppliers and are operated by Digicel and LIME. If you bring your own phone from home you can choose whether to select Digicel or LIME networks. The LIME (Landline, Internet, Mobile, Entertainment) office on Bridge Street in Castries, near the post office, has public telephones and sells a wide selection of phonecards. Both Digicel and LIME have offices in Baywalk Mall, Rodney Bay. There are internet cafes and facilities throughout the island, in the resort areas and in shopping centres. Most hotels have computers for guests' use and internet access for those with laptops, tablets and smart phones.

TIME ZONES

Four hours behind Greenwich Mean Time in the winter, five hours when Daylight Saving Time applies.

TIPPING

Be prepared to pay a 10 percent service charge and 8 percent government tax on all goods and services supplied by hotels and restaurants. In particular most restaurants and hotels will often automatically add a 10–15percent service charge to your bill, so no further gratuity is necessary unless you would like to tip an especially attentive waiter or another member of staff. Where service is not included a tip of 10–20 percent is appropriate. Porters, chambermaids and taxi drivers expect a tip.

TOILETS

Toilets can be found in shopping malls, the cruise ship complexes, tourist sites, hotels and restaurants.

TOURIST INFORMATION

The St Lucia Tourist Board's website is www.stlucia.org, http://stlucianow.co.uk or http://stlucianow.com. The Tourist Board's administrative office is in Castries (PO Box 221, Sureline Building, Vide Bouteille, Castries, tel: 758-452 4094), but there are information booths at Hewanorra and George F.L. Charles airports,

Pointe Seraphine and Place Carenage seaports in Castries.

For information about the island before you travel, visit the below tourist board offices:

Canada, 60 St. Clair Avenue East, Suite 909, Toronto, Ontario M4T 1N5, tel: (416) 362 4242

UK, 1 Collingham Gardens, London SW5 0HW, tel: 020 7341 7005

USA, 800 Second Avenue, 9th Floor, Suite 910, New York, NY 10017, tel: (212) 867 2951/2950

TRANSPORT

Buses. The public bus system in St Lucia operates from early in the morning until early evening. It is safe to say that more buses run in the morning and that the frequency tends to tail off after the end of the working day. Castries and Vieux Fort have the best services, but the more remote rural areas aren't always as well served. If you go to Soufrière by bus, it is usually quicker and easier to return via Vieux Fort, where there are better connections.

Buses can be distinguished from other minibuses by their licence plates, which begin with the letter M. The routes are zoned and priced accordingly, so a short hop costs EC$1.50, while a longer trip from Castries to Soufrière costs EC$8; you must have the exact fare.

In Castries, buses for the north of the island leave from a terminus behind the market on Darling Road; buses for Anse la Raye and the west coast road leave from the south side of the market; buses for Dennery and Vieux Fort leave from Hospital Road by the river.

If you do travel on the bus you will hear local people call out "one stop" when they want to get off. Once you are familiar with the route, you could try it yourself. Alternatively, ask the driver to let you know when you reach your destination.

Taxis. Taxis are available in the form of a saloon vehicle or a minivan that can accommodate a small group. They are plentiful at the airports, in the resort areas at hotels, at shopping malls and in town at the official stands. Look for the TX licence plate. Taxis are not metered because fares are fixed and the majority of drivers tend to stick to the published rates. However, check the fare before setting off and make sure you are being quoted in EC dollars. A taxi from Rodney Bay to Gros Islet costs EC$25 (US$10), from Castries to Soufrière EC$239 (US$90), Castries to Vieux Fort EC$199 (US$75).

A taxi is the obvious choice for a hotel transfer to and from the airport, unless your hotel offers a shuttle service. You can also arrange for a taxi driver/guide to take you on an island tour, on a shopping trip, or on an excursion to the Friday Night fish fry at Anse La Raye and the Jump-up at Gros Islet. Reliable and knowledgeable local drivers are affiliated to the following associations:

North Lime Taxi Association, Rodney Bay, tel: 758-452 8562; email: nltaxi@hotmail.com

Soufrière Taxi Association, tel: 758-459 5562; www.soufrieretaxi.com

Southern Taxi Association, Hewanorra International Airport, Vieux Fort, tel: 758-454 6136; www.southerntaxi.com

V

VISAS AND ENTRY REQUIREMENTS

Passports are required for entry to St Lucia, except for British, French, Canadian and US citizens on short visits (weekend to one week) holding return tickets. US citizens do however need a passport for re-entry into the US and passports are highly recommended for ease of access into St Lucia for everyone. For visa requirements, other information and updates, see www.stlucia.gov.lc.

Customs. Visitors may take the following into St Lucia duty-free: 40 fl ozs (1.18 litres) of alcohol (travellers aged 18 and up only)

200 cigarettes or 50 cigars or 2kg of smoking tobacco
Gifts and souvenirs of a value less than $270
Personal effects

WEBSITES

http://stlucianow.com The official St Lucia tourist site with information on how to get there, where to stay, how to get around and what to do while you're there.

www.gov.uk/foreign-travel-advice/st-lucia Travel advice from the British Foreign and Commonwealth Office, including safety, security and health alerts.

www.slunatrust.org The St Lucia National Trust has a number of protected sites, details of which are on this website.

http://forestryeeunit.blogspot.co.uk The Forestry Department maintains the forest trails and protects wildlife on St Lucia. This blog by the Environmental Education Unit contains news and information as well as contact details for all the trails.

www.heritagetoursstlucia.org Details of the many Heritas sites around St Lucia can be found on the website.

WEDDINGS

St Lucia has long been a popular destination for getting married abroad, as well as for honeymoons. Marrying overseas allows couples to combine the wedding and honeymoon, and even bring friends and relations along too.

Couples can opt to have their nuptials barefoot on the beach, in a small island church, or at a national landmark, such as Diamond Botanical Gardens, Pigeon Island National Landmark or at the foot of the Pitons. All provide wonderful and picturesque backdrops to a big day.

Tour operators in the UK and USA offer all-inclusive wedding and honeymoon packages, while larger hotels have a dedicated wedding planner, who can arrange every detail, whether it's a simple ceremony or a lavish family affair.

At present, same-sex unions are not possible on St Lucia.

There is no residency period for getting married on St Lucia, but you will need to apply for a Same Day Marriage License ($200) and have all the required paperwork to hand (see below). If you do not require the license immediately, you can apply for a regular Marriage License ($125). The process is well-established and should be straightforward, leaving the happy couple to get on with planning their day.

Documents required before the wedding can take place are:

A valid passport

Birth certificate

Divorcees should bring their Decree Absolute

Widows/widowers should bring the death certificate of their spouse and also their original marriage certificate

A deed poll is required if there has been a name change

If the bride or groom is under 18 the parents must provide their consent in a sworn affidavit stamped by a Notary Public.

RECOMMENDED HOTELS

People who stay in Castries are usually business travellers who need to be in the city. The north of the island is traditionally the place for beach resorts and package holidays, with a wide range of restaurants in and around Rodney Bay, which is also a magnet for those on yachts wanting a good marina. The southwest coast, around Soufrière is the most beautiful part of the island, with spectacular views of the Pitons, picturesque bays and forested mountains in which to hike and watch birds.

Off-season rates (mid-April to mid-December) can be substantially lower than high-season rates (mid-December to mid-April). Be prepared to pay a 10 percent service charge and a government tax of 10 percent, but for all-inclusive package holidays this may already be included in the price you are quoted. Rates are subject to change, so always check in advance.

The price categories quoted below are for a double room a night in high season, excluding tax and service.

$$$$	above US$300
$$$	US$200–300
$$	US$100–200
$	under US$100

CASTRIES

Auberge Seraphine $$ *Vielle Bay, Pointe Seraphine, Castries, tel: 758-453 2073; www.aubergeseraphine.com.* Small city hotel close to George F.L. Charles Airport and central Castries. Simple accommodation with view of the harbour. Swimming pool and beach shuttle.

Eudovic Guest House $ *Goodlands, Castries, tel: 758-452 2747; email: eudovic@candw.lc.* Small, friendly guesthouse run by local artist and woodcarver Vincent Eudovic and his family. Ten minutes from Castries' centre. Rooms are simple with lovely furniture made from local wood, a kitchenette and fan. The artist's studio is at the same property.

Rendezvous Resort $$$$ *Malabar Beach, tel: 758-452 4211;* www. theromanticholiday.com. Couples-only, all-inclusive, medium-sized hotel set in pretty gardens with friendly staff. Cool beachfront and garden suites, spa, swimming pool and whirlpool. The beach is lovely but close to the centre of Castries and alongside George F.L. Charles Airport.

NORTH OF CASTRIES

Calabash Cove Resort & Spa $$$$ *Bonaire Estate, Marisule, tel: 758-456 3500;* www.calabashcove.com. Quiet, delightful small hotel of rooms and suites on hillside and waterfront. Cottages on the water are large, wood-panelled suites with vine-covered deck, plunge pool, outdoor shower, hammocks and every luxury going. Rooms in the main building are smaller but well-appointed. Excellent food (allinclusive packages available but all meals are à la carte), impeccable service and lush gardens.

East Winds $$$$ *Labrelotte Bay, tel: 758-452 8212;* www.eastwinds. com. Small intimate, all-inclusive beachfront hotel with views of Labrelotte Bay and stylish cottage accommodation with 30 pretty rooms. This is a long-established hotel in lovely tropical gardens with gourmet restaurant and piano bar. Rates include four meals, snacks, all drinks and watersports equipment.

Villa Beach Cottages $$$–$$$$ *Choc Bay, tel: 758-450 2884;* www. villabeachcottages.com. Self-catering cottages and suites on Choc Bay. Spacious rooms with air-conditioning, some with four poster beds, all with kitchens. Water sports facilities and pool. You can rent additional equipment from the Sandals Resort next door. The sister property, **Dauphine Estate**, at Etangs, Soufrière, offers a two-centre experience, with plantation life complementing the beach.

RODNEY BAY

Bay Gardens Resorts $$–$$$$ *Rodney Bay, tel: 457 8006;* www. baygardensresorts.com. There are three hotels in this locally owned group, all in Rodney Bay and popular with business and leisure travellers alike. The most luxurious is the Bay Gardens Beach Resort, an all-suite hotel right on Reduit Beach with spa, fitness centre, car hire, dive shop and watersports. Bay Gardens Hotel and the smaller Bay Gardens Inn are in the heart of the village close to the road to Gros Islet. They have comfortable rooms and a high rate of repeat visitors, reflecting their popularity.

Coco Palm $$–$$$ *Rodney Bay Boulevard, tel: 758-456 2800;* www. coco-resorts.com. Stylish mid-sized hotel in the village, a great location convenient for beach, nightlife and shopping, but set back from the road to eliminate noise. Comfortable rooms and suites overlook the pool or garden, the best being on the ground floor with French doors giving direct access to a patio and the pool.

Ginger Lily $$–$$$ *Reduit Beach, tel: 758-458 0300;* www.theginger lilyhotel.com. Small hotel across the road from Reduit Beach. Quiet, with simple spacious rooms, continental breakfast included, small pool and lovely gardens.

Harmony Suites $$–$$$ *Rodney Bay, tel: 758-452 8756;* www.harmony suites.com. Comfortable, moderately priced suite accommodation near Reduit Beach with views of the marina; no children under 12. Meal plans available but there is more variety at local restaurants.

NORTH COAST

Cap Maison $$$$ *Smuggler's Cove Drive, Cap Estate, tel: 758-457 8670;* www.capmaison.com. Luxury rooms, suites and villa suites with full kitchens in clifftop boutique hotel overlooking Smuggler's Cove. Spacious, comfortable, good facilities and attentive service. Panoramic views to Pigeon Point from the much-praised Cliff at Cap restaurant. Beach bar for daytime snacks, beach towels and water sports.

Cotton Bay Village $$$–$$$$ *Cas-en-Bas, tel: 758-456 5700;* www. cottonbaystlucia.com. A compact development on the Atlantic coast but safe for swimming. Suites, townhouses and villas consisting of one to four bedrooms, many with their own private pools, while the most expensive have the luxury of 24-hour butler service. The resort is within walking distance of the golf course but remote from other amenities.

La Panache $ *Cas-en-Bas Road, Gros Islet, tel: 758-715 6910;* www.saintlucianplants.com/lapanache. A guest house with three simple, air-conditioned, self-catering apartments on a hillside with views from the balconies over Rodney Bay and Pigeon Island. Clean, friendly, relaxed and quiet, with lovely garden. For a two-centre holiday, the owner has another apartment in the south, between Laborie and Choiseul, overlooking a ravine with views of Gros Piton.

The bodyholiday LeSport $$$$ *Cariblue Beach, Cap Estate, tel: 758-457 7800;* www.thebodyholiday.com. A luxury, all-inclusive spa resort in the far north of the island set on a hillside with a palm-shaded beach; suites are spacious and tastefully furnished for couples or singles. Lots of activities and sports, from archery to yoga. The restaurants serve great food and there is live entertainment. Staff are friendly and give excellent service.

MARIGOT BAY

Capella Marigot Bay $$$$ *Marigot Bay, tel: 758-458 5300;* www.capellahotels.com/saintlucia. Luxury resort on the hillside running down to the waterfront, lovely views of the harbour and the yachts, with every amenity. Gourmet restaurants and boutique shops at The Marina Village, as well as water sports at the marina.

The Inn On The Bay $$$ *Marigot Bay, tel: 758-451 4260;* www.saint-lucia.com. A small bed & breakfast inn on the hilltop with a glorious view over the bay, run by generous and welcoming hosts who can arrange activities. Comfortable rooms have fans and verandas which catch the breezes. Free shuttle to the bay area.

JJ's Paradise Resort $–$$ *Marigot Bay, tel: 758-451 4761;* www.jjsparadise.com. A popular St Lucian-owned and operated resort and restaurant on a hillside close to sheltered Marigot Bay. Clean, spacious standard rooms, or air-conditioned suites and cottages with verandas overlooking the bay. Friendly and helpful staff.

Ti Kaye Village Resort $$$–$$$$ *Anse Cochon, tel: 758-456 8101;* www.tikaye.com. Remote hideaway on a cliffside south of Anse la Raye. Romantic Caribbean-style cottages. The beach is a short walk down and a long walk up 169 steps. Popular with honeymooners and a good choice for divers; the *Lesleen M* shipwreck is just offshore. The clifftop spa uses only locally made, natural products.

SOUFRIÈRE

Anse Chastanet and Jade Mountain $$$–$$$$ *Soufrière, tel: 758-459 7000;* www.ansechastanet.com, www.jademountainstlucia. com. Lovely, stylish and spacious, open-sided but private accommodation set on a hillside with breathtaking views of the Pitons, sea and forest. The Jade Mountain suites on the hilltop are modern, fabulously luxurious, romantic and breezy, each with its own infinity pool. Excellent restaurants and a lovely spa for pampering, with diving, mountain biking, tennis, yoga, kayaking and other watersports available. The resort has a volcanic sand beach, but nearby Anse Mamin has a stretch of fine white sand.

Crystals $$$–$$$$ *Soufrière, tel: 758-384 8995;* www.stluciacrystals. com. Five rustic, quirky self-catering cottages with colourful décor and homely feel are a mixture of North African and plantation house style, with artwork scattered in every corner. Rooms all have a view of the Pitons, plunge pool, swimming pool or Jacuzzi. The Tree House bar and restaurant is available for guests only, picnic lunches are available and help with excursions offered.

Fond Doux Plantation & Resort $$$$ *Soufrière, tel: 758-459 7545;* www.fonddouxestate.com. Pretty, traditional chattel houses remodelled as comfortable guest accommodation on this working cocoa plantation. Peaceful countryside location set in tropical gardens around a French colonial estate house. Relaxing, charming, helpful staff and good food with ingredients from the estate.

Boucan (Hotel Chocolat) $$$$ *Rabot Estate, Soufrière, tel: UK: +44 (0)3444 932323, US: +1-758-572-9600;* www.thehotelchocolat.com. Boutique hotel and restaurant of traditional-style wooden cottages and villas on a working cocoa estate with views of the Pitons. Clean lines with white linen and every luxury and comfort. You can take pleasant walks on the estate through fruit trees to historic battle sites, or tours of the cocoa plantation. Spa offers massages using local cocoa nibs, oil and butter.

Sugar Beach $$$$ *Val des Pitons, Jalousie Bay, tel: 758-456 8000;* www.viceroyhotelsandresorts.com/sugarbeach. Luxury resort on lush former plantation extending back from a sheltered bay between the Pitons. Villas are in tasteful clusters each with a butler, every comfort and absolute privacy. As well as tennis, a PADI dive centre and children's activities, the rainforest spa has treehouse gazebos built among the ruins of the old sugar plantation. Delicious food is offered in the restaurants while the ultra-modern, pop-art Cane Bar stocks specialty rums.

La Haut Plantation $$$–$$$$ *West Coast Road, Soufrière, tel: 758-459 7008;* www.lahaut.com. A family-run guesthouse with spacious rooms and private balcony from which to enjoy a stunning view of the Pitons. Not on the beach but with a fabulous infinity pool. A self-contained cottage is also available to rent. Good restaurant and great breakfasts.

Ladera Resort $$$$ *Soufrière, tel: 758-459 7323;* www.ladera. com. Upscale and exclusive hillside property of villas and suites 3km (2 miles) from the centre of Soufrière. Rooms, crafted from stone and rich hardwood, are open on one side with private plunge pools. Lovely tropical gardens and breathtaking views over Soufrière Bay to the Pitons; excellent cuisine at the award-winning Dasheene Restaurant. Spa treatments and warm mineral pools for bathing.

Stonefield Estate Resort $$$$ *Soufrière, tel: 758-459 7037;* www. stonefieldvillas.com. Small villa complex in beautifully landscaped gardens almost 2km (1.2 mile) from Soufrière. Each villa has 1–3 bedrooms and is individual; some have a garden shower, a veranda and panoramic views of the Pitons, the sea and Soufrière. Swimming pool, a good restaurant and a spa which uses local products, including home-grown cocoa.

VIEUX FORT AND THE SOUTH

Balenbouche Estate $$ *between Laborie and Choiseul, tel: 758-455 1244;* www.balenbouche.com. Family-run guesthouse with colonial-style self-catering cottages to rent on an 18thcentury sugar plantation that remains a working organic farm. A popular heritage site (see page 72) with tropical gardens, containing huge old trees and machinery from the sugar mill including an old water wheel; it is used for weddings and yoga retreats. Friendly, intimate, with a rustic, faded-glory feel. Delicious home-cooked food available.

Mirage Beach $–$$ *Laborie, tel: 758-455 9237;* www.miragestlucia. com. Right on the beach, this small, rustic hotel in a fishing community is quiet and away from the tourist hustle. Two-bedroom apartment upstairs and master bedroom downstairs, both with kitchenettes. There are good local restaurants in the village or meals can be prepared for you in your apartment by local cooks.

The Reef Beach Huts $ *Anse de Sables, tel: 758-454 3418,* www.slucia. com/reef. A few rustic wooden huts tucked behind the popular café on the beach. Ideal for windsurfers and kitesurfers who don't mind basic lodgings. Fans and mosquito nets are provided and breakfast on the beach is included.

EAST COAST

Fox Grove Inn $ *Mon Repos, Micoud, tel: 758-455 3271;* www.fox groveinn.com. Small country hotel close to Mamiku Gardens. The 12 simple guestrooms and self-contained apartments have en suite showers or bathrooms and ceiling fans. Surrounded by banana and coconut plantations with good views of Praslin Bay and excellent pool. Good restaurant on site.

INDEX

INSIGHT ⊙ GUIDES POCKET GUIDE

ST LUCIA

First Edition 2016

Written by Sarah Cameron
Edited by Sarah Clark
Cartography by Carte
Picture Editor: Tom Smyth
Photography credits: Alamy 6BL, 7BL, 39, 54,
63, 77; ATV Paradise Tours 92; Chris Huxley/
Rain Forest Adventures 9TC, 46; Corbis 5M,
7MC, 48, 74, 101, 106; Dreamstime 59, 72; FLPA
4ML, 81; Getty Images 4TC, 4ML, 5M, 9TC, 11,
18, 20, 22, 33, 44, 60, 68, 69, 71, 84, 91, 102;
iStock 4TL, 4MC, 5T, 5M, 5M, 6ML, 6MR, 6TL,
6TL, 6M, 7T, 8TL, 8TR, 13, 14, 24, 26, 28/29, 31,
32, 35, 37, 40, 41, 42, 49, 53, 56, 62, 65, 66, 67,
70, 76, 79, 83, 86, 89, 90, 96, 98, 105, 108; Mary
Evans Picture Library19; Public domain 16, 17;
Robert Harding 50; Saint Lucia Tourist Board
36, 45, 61, 78, 80, 87, 88, 94; SuperStock 82
Cover picture: Getty Images

Distribution

UK, Ireland and Europe: Apa Publications
(UK) Ltd; sales@insightguides.com
United States and Canada: Ingram Publisher
Services; ips@ingramcontent.com
Australia and New Zealand: Woodslane;
info@woodslane.com.au
Southeast Asia: Apa Publications (SN) Pte;
singaporeoffice@insightguides.com
Hong Kong, Taiwan and China:
Apa Publications (HK) Ltd;
hongkongoffice@insightguides.com

Worldwide: Apa Publications (UK) Ltd;
sales@insightguides.com

Special Sales, Content Licensing and CoPublishing

Insight Guides can be purchased in bulk
quantities at discounted prices. We can create
special editions, personalised jackets and
corporate imprints tailored to your needs.
sales@insightguides.com;
www.insightguides.biz

All Rights Reserved
© 2016 Apa Digital (CH) AG and
Apa Publications (UK) Ltd

Printed in China by CTPS

No part of this book may be reproduced,
stored in a retrieval system or transmitted in
any form or means electronic, mechanical,
photocopying, recording or otherwise,
without prior written permission from
Apa Publications.

Contact us

Every effort has been made to provide
accurate information in this publication,
but changes are inevitable. The publisher
cannot be responsible for any resulting loss,
inconvenience or injury. We would appreciate
it if readers would call our attention to any
errors or outdated information. We also
welcome your suggestions; please contact us
at: hello@insightguides.com
www.insightguides.com